Gun Dog Training--
Do It Yourself And
Do It Right

by Len Jenkins

Published by:
CJ Publications
3260 Sheick Road
Monroe, Michigan 48161

ISBN Number 0-9628712-2-2
price $18.95

D1595880

Gun Dog Training--
Do It Yourself And
Do It Right!

Effective strategies for developing
a personal gun dog who hunts with
style, discipline, and spirit

by Len Jenkins

CJ Publications, Monroe, Michigan

Whether you think you can or think you can't, you're right.

- Henry Ford

About The Author

Len Jenkins has been raising English setters, conducting gun dog clinics and seminars, and training gun dogs for several years on his farm in Monroe County, Michigan. Since his youth he has hunted grouse and woodcock in Michigan's Tittabawassee Forest. He has never been far from a bird dog, having owned setters, pointers, and German shorthaired pointers over the years.

A high school and college English and biology teacher by profession, Len earned his B.A. from Central Michigan University and M.A. in literature from Eastern Michigan University. He has taken postgraduate work in environmental science and water resource management at the University of Michigan. Interested in outdoor writing, he writes articles on gun dog training and related subjects for national publication.

Len continues to hunt, raise English setters, train gun dogs of all sporting breeds, and promote wildlife preservation and conservation through habitat maintenance. He conducts individual gun dog training sessions and seminars at his training grounds in both Monroe and Midland Counties, Michigan.

Dedication

To my loving wife, Char, for being kind enough to tell me all the things I didn't want to hear. Her inspiration, support, encouragement, ideas, hard work, and commitment were instrumental in making this book a reality.

Disclaimer

This book was written as a guide for the individual wishing to train his or her own gun dog. The methods and philosphy advanced herein have worked for the author in training gun dogs of various breeds. The concept inherent to the premise of this book is that the owner should develop a close relationship with his own dog and perform all training in a logical manner consistent with the dog's individual nature as well as the desired outcome.

Each dog requires consideration as an individual just as each person requires individual consideration. Some techniques work for some people but not for others. By the same token, what is effective with one dog may not be with another. Therefore, careful assessment of each person's strengths and weaknesses and each dog's ability to absorb training must be made. The author works with individuals and their dogs and has noted many differences in temperament of both owners and dogs. The author also believes that most problems in dogs are caused by inept, inconsistent, emotional, or inadequate training. The author and C J Publications urge you to assess yourself as well as your dog. You are urged to read as much as possible on the subject and seek the advice of professional gun dog trainers should your efforts fail to achieve the desired results.

Realizing the individual vagaries of both owner and dog, neither the author nor the publisher shall assume any responsibility or liability to any individual or entity relative to any damage or loss caused, or alleged to have been caused, directly or indirectly, by the methods, techniques, procedures, and corrections contained herein.

The purpose of this book is to inform, help, guide, and entertain. In presenting the material, careful attention was given to text as well as implication from text. Nowhere in this book is harm intended to any entity. Further, in order to follow conventional syntax and assure readability, the masculine pronouns he, him, and his were used consistently in a generic sense to refer to all human beings. There is no place for sexism in modern society and none was intended here.

Every effort was made to make this book technically accurate although there may be errors, both typographical and content, for which the author assumes no responsibility. Photo credit was given to each person who contributed photos he presumably took and gave to the author for inclusion in this book. The author and publisher assume no responsibility for additional compensation, consideration, or credit for said photographs.

Acknowledgements

Many fine sportsmen and women have influenced the writing of this book but none more than my wife, Char, who has spent countless hours typing and editing the manuscript and kept me on course with her encouragement and inspiration.

Others have also contributed to the final product, having had meaningful impact in many ways. These special friends include Bill Bolyard, Gordon and Valrie Lewis, Brad Belanger, Frank and Christine Tabone, Dick Geswein, Bob Andre, Preston Crabtree, Bob and Darla Naylor, John Karpinski, Tim and Eve Bryson, the McDermids, John Laney and son, John, Rapheal Lieto, and Randy Mapus, who contributed photographs and provided help and moral support.

A very special thank you also goes to Terry Krueger, Dan Wizner, Ed Polk, Cyril Keiffer, Paul Carson and William E. McCloskey, Ph.D. Terry, a professional photographer from LaSalle, Michigan, took the close-up photos of the dog training equipment and Dan took the pictures of the Tittabawassee Forest grouse hunt. Ed, an artist whose work I admire, has provided the illustrations which grace the pages of this volume. Cyril, through his generosity and skill at desk-top publishing, was instrumental in transforming this book into the finished product. Paul, Director of Information and Editor of the Ruffed Grouse Society, has provided the photographs of the ruffed grouse in their natural habitat. Bill, a colleague for whom I have always had great respect, proofread the manuscript and offered invaluable advice and suggestions.

My children, Danielle, Michael, Anne, and Elizabeth have contributed immensely through their tolerance, encouragement, and willingness to relieve me of some of my chores around the kennel while I wrote.

I owe a debt of gratitude to the late Claude Turpin and his very gracious wife, Ruth. They introduced me to the pleasures of English setters many years ago and instilled in me an appreciation for hunting with fine sporting dogs.

And last, though by no means least, Bill, my English setter who always positioned himself near me as I wrote, thumping his tail approvingly as the writing of this book evolved from an idea to the tangible text you have before you.

Thanks to all!

Table of Contents

Chapter..**Page #**

Foreword...xi
Introduction xiii

1 Put Yourself in the Picture 2
2 Buying a Dog.....................................6
3 Bringing Home a New Puppy 11
4 The Breeds.......................................19
5 You and Your Pup: How About a Partnership?.....26
6 A Dog's Limited Working Vocabulary 31
7 Gun Dog Jargon...................................36
8 Predictability 44
9 Consistency......................................49
10 Needed: The Right Attitude 52
11 Realistic Goal Setting 55
12 Everything Is Training............................58
13 Thirty Thoughts Worth Remembering...............62
14 The Right Tools for Effective Training............65
15 Training 74
16 Correcting Faults 111
17 The Shock Collar 151
18 Dealing with Shyness 158
19 Shooting Preserves 162
20 Beauty -- More than Skin Deep 166
21 Do You Like Your Dog?...........................170

Chapter..**Page #**

22 A Written Program, Schedule, and Evaluation 172
23 Weather or Not 177
24 Buying an Older Dog 181
25 Grouse Dogs.. 186
26 Training with Pigeons 191
27 The FDSB 196
28 The AKC 200
29 Today's English Setter.................................. 204
30 The Environmental Factor:
        Top Performance More Than Luck 210
31 Home Quail Covey.. 215
32 The Quarry 219
33 Save Our Sport.. 232

        Afterword 237
        Appendix I.. 239
        Appendix II 240
        Appendix III 242
        Index.. 245

Foreword

I envy anyone who doubts the value of a book such as this. A doubter would have to be a person with a lot of leisure time. Then he could dabble in dog training, or whatever he chooses, until he gets it right.

Dabbling is a lost art for most of us. We don't have time to experiment and often have to rely for our satisfaction on the work of someone who has provided a clear trail for us to follow.

Len Jenkins, a veteran dog trainer, has spent most of his adult life refining methods--some of them rather sneaky--to convince four-legged students that the greatest fun in the world is learning to become gun dogs. He presents here a guide to anyone who dreams of watching his own personally trained gun dog work. Admittedly, considering all of the horror stories making the rounds, a potential do-it-yourself dog trainer might at first fear a nightmare rather than anticipate a dream-come-true. But *Gun Dog Training--Do It Yourself and Do It Right!* leaves nothing to chance. It provides a plan and the details to make the plan work.

All interaction with your dog is training, Len believes, and sets the stage for a campaign designed to train a gun dog as a natural extension of the friendship between dog and owner. So, take a close look at the relationship between you and your dog before you start, Len advises. And if the two of you like each other, you've made a great start.

The upland hunting experience is more than fine dog work, of course. And among the subjects mentioned in the book that Len feels should be important to hunters is being actively involved in the conservation of upland game birds.

But the centerpiece of the book is the making of a stylish, disciplined and spirited gun dog. In its own way, such a hunting companion capable of finding and retrieving cripples is an asset to conservation.

But before a gun dog can perform satisfactorily in the field, a stint of training is essential. How efficiently that training progresses depends on a lot of variables. And by opening this book you've taken a significant step to cut down considerably on many of the variables blocking success.

Samuel R. Pursglove, Jr.
Executive Director,
The Ruffed Grouse Society
Coraopolis, Pennsylvania

Introduction

Y ou can enjoy hunting with a finished gun dog that *does it all* and does it in high style. Since every bird brought down by the gun will be retrieved to hand, you'll feel good about your commitment to conservation and sportsman-like hunting. You'll have the satisfaction of knowing that you personally developed a first-class gun dog that will devote his energies to hunting for you. Through commitment and dedication, you will have a dog that you'll be proud to own.

Training a bird dog is enjoyable, but you have to think before you act. You must formulate a plan, a strategy, and then work that plan. You have to map out a workable course of action ahead of time. In order to get somewhere you have to know where you're going. In order to achieve success, you must have a goal and be willing to devote the time and effort to work *smart*. If you know what you want and if you develop a strategy for achieving it, you'll succeed.

Before you start, analyze both your dog and yourself. If you think your dog has what it takes to become a suitable gun dog, you're half way there. Then analyze yourself. If you possess such traits as patience, dedication, and kindness, you'll be off to a good start. Combine this with your basic knowledge of the sport of hunting and you'll realize great satisfaction in training your own personal gun dog.

This book will be your guide and will provide you with the information, training techniques, suggestions, and tried-and true-methods which you can use in your training program.

Putting together a jigsaw puzzle and training a dog are very similar. Each piece in the puzzle is an integral part of the whole and the picture is not complete until each piece is interlocked into the finished composition. Training a dog also involves working with one piece at a time, fitting it into the whole.

In order to complete your training jigsaw puzzle, you will need a sound strategy for achieving your goal. This strategy can be compared to an equation which involves four vital parts which yield a finished product when added together. Think about it as you do your training:

Patience + forethought + common sense +

honest effort = a finished gun dog.

By putting this equation into practice, you'll also be proud of your efforts, knowing that you possess the character and virtues necessary to accomplish something important. You'll have the satisfaction of making your dog a personal gun dog in the truest sense.

If you really want to train your own gun dog, you can. If you lack experience, don't worry about it. Just take the time necessary to analyze what it is you really want. If you want a finished gun dog, you'll have one. You can do it. As you read this book, think about it in terms of your dog as well as your personal goals and aspirations. If you are consistent, persistent and insistent, you will develop a polished, high-class gun dog that *does it all*. Success is at hand; let's get started!

Photo 1 by: Dan Wizner

An excellent Tittabawassee Forest woodcock covert.

1

Put Yourself In The Picture

Imagine yourself in this picture, hunting the elusive grouse in Michigan's Tittabawassee Forest. It's a spectacular crisp fall morning with the early sun rays glinting off the frost-encrystalled vegetation. As we park the truck at the side of the winding fire lane, we know this is going to be one of those special morning hunts which will leave an indelible mark on the memory. Let's free my setters, Bill and Smokey, from their travel crates where they also are anticipating an exciting and memorable hunt. Well, here it goes. Let's cut east off this two-track and follow the edge of that clear cut section over the sand hill to the alder swamp. Then we'll follow the edge between the blueberry marsh and mature aspen stand. With all that varied cover laden with seeds, nuts, buds, and berries on the forest floor, we should find grouse. And if we fail, we can always hunt the alders in search of woodcock.

Photo 2 by: Dan Wizner.
Charlen's Bill Crockett and Charlen's Smokey coursing the Tittabawassee in quest of grouse and woodcock.

As we enter the woods, Bill and Smoke quarter powerfully in front, eacn apparently oblivious to his brace mate's presence as they sift the air currents for grouse scent. The dogs are stunning, with proud heads held high and tails cracking, bounding over and through vegetative obstacles in their quest of a reason for a productive point. The bells are cheerfully ringing, a music of sorts in this frosty forest amphitheater. Suddenly one bell is silent. Then the other! The dogs are locked on point just behind that thin screen of

Photo 3 by: Dan Wizner.
The Tittabawassee Forest -- good grouse country is best enjoyed with good grouse dogs.

saplings. Bill's in front. Rigid. Tail frozen high. Smoke's about twenty feet behind, honoring the point. As we proceed we'll have to be ready for the exploding bird. The anticipation is building. This is definitely not for the faint-hearted! The dogs know the bird is here, so we'll cautiously go in to flush, knowing the quarry probably is thirty to forty feet in front of Bill's radar nose. Get set! There he goes! A whir of wings and blinding speed penetrate the still, crisp air. We'll make the shot instinctively as the bird rockets through the tree tops. The bird has been dropped in the brackens, and both dogs torpedo to the marked fall. Smoke gets there first and picks up the prize. Then he brings it in, releasing it to hand, proud of his effort and pleased that we're sharing this magnificent morning hunt with him and Bill in one of our favorite coverts.

The Tittabawassee is a very special place to me, a place I've hunted as a boy and return to faithfully each fall. This is a place of cherished memories of hunting. This area is where

Photo 4 by Dan Wizner.

The writer and Smokey take a moment to enjoy a favorite grouse covert in Midland County, Michigan.

my dad introduced me to grouse hunting, and I in turn introduced my own son to the same sport.

But you probably have your own favorite haunts. Perhaps it's in grouse country, a southern pine forest, Midwest farm fields, or the Canadian prairie. Wherever it is, picture yourself there, hunting your favorite game bird with a spectacular gun dog working out in front, doing his utmost to produce game for the gun and doing it in high style, not because he has to but because he thrives on the sport. Envision such a dog, a flawless master of his art. Imagine your satisfaction knowing you've developed your canine protege into the artful, classy sporting dog you see before you. Visualize the perfect autumn day hunting your favorite game bird with a dog as near to perfection as possible, working hard but making it look easy because he derives incredible joy from the sport.

Well, you can have a finished gun dog to complete this imaginary picture. And you'll have a fine time in developing a class dog as you use this book as a guide. Put yourself in the fall setting of your choice with a fine dog in front doing all you expect and doing it in electrifying high style. You can have such a dog. You can have it all--the style, the class, the energy, the excitement, and the high-quality time afield--behind a superb gun dog.

Grouse hunting is best enjoyed with a grouse dog!

2

Buying A Dog

Because you're probably going to have your dog for a long time, buying a gun dog requires forethought. Many sportspeople approach this matter very casually and consult only the encyclopedia regarding breeds of sporting dogs and only the classified section of the local newspaper regarding availability. It's no wonder that so many people end up with the wrong information, the wrong breed, and the wrong dog.

All sporting breeds are not equal. Some are generally better than others although there are excellent individuals in all breeds. A good dog of a rare breed, for instance, is a good gun dog in its own right, not because it is representative of its breed but rather because it's a good dog. Period. A show-style English setter or a pointer might be a good bird dog, as an individual, but not just because it's a setter or pointer developed for show. No. A good dog is a good dog. But if

Photo 5 by: Paul Carson.

Grouse are the gamebird supreme of the Tittabawassee Forest!

you want to maximize your chances of acquiring a suitable field dog, don't gamble. Go to sources in which field performance is stressed in breeding. Go to an individual or kennel which can articulate what is being bred. If you're interested in field trials, go to a kennel or breeder specializing in trial dogs. If you're interested in a show champion, go to a kennel or individual specializing in show dogs. But if you're a hunter, make no mistake about where you should look for a good gun dog--go to a kennel or individual who breeds tractable, durable, athletic, birdy dogs that want to hunt.

There are many considerations. Make inquiries when buying a dog. You might confer with friends or associates who know something regarding a reputable kennel. National sporting magazines usually carry advertisements for kennels that have made a commitment to producing quality gun dogs. Although there is a good chance you'll locate a good litter of pups close to home, you might also have to travel to get exactly what you want. Your local newspaper's classified section might carry advertisements which will lead you to what you're looking for. It might also lead you to *junk* dogs or dogs of a breeding program unsuitable for the field. Make your inquiries, but be selective. Consider all your options regarding purchase of a gun dog.

The reputation of the breeder is important. There are honest as well as unscrupulous individuals in all endeavors. Is the breeder from whom you're considering buying a dog one who enjoys a good reputation? Does he seem honest? Does it appear that he's made a commitment? Chances are that if he appears to be "wheeling and dealing," if he negotiates price easily, or if he tries to talk you into a breed you didn't want, he very possibly lacks integrity or good repute. Ask the breeder about the parents and grandparents of the dog you're considering. Ask about a written guarantee, including the specifics of what's covered. Does the breeder provide the necessary registration papers and extended pedigree? Does he offer any training services? Are his dogs properly immunized, dewormed, healthy and well cared for? Does he seem sincere? If you *smell a rat*, don't buy. There are enough honest, reputable breeders around so don't get stuck with a problem because you don't want to actively search out the right prospect. Just because a kennel is geographically close doesn't mean it's the right kennel for you, although it could be. Check into things. It's every bit as important to buy from the right breeder as it is to buy the right dog.

Price is sometimes a consideration. If you can't afford a quality dog, keep looking and something suitable might eventually come along at a price you can afford. But if you're serious about what you want, you should expect to pay a fair price. After all, good gun dog breeding programs don't spring up haphazardly over night. Look for an individual who has made a commitment to producing quality dogs. There's an old expression that goes, *You get what you pay for.* It's so true in many areas, and gun dogs are no exception. If you want something good, be prepared to pay a fair price for it although there are even pitfalls after accepting this notion. For instance, you might visit two kennels. One is a kennel

Photo 6 by: Dan Wizner.
Plep, a superb grouse dog, trained by Dan Wizner of Bay City, Michigan, relishes the fruits of her day's labor--two Tittabawassee grouse. Seasoned grouse dogs like Plep are hard to find at any price!

specializing in *show quality* dogs of some fairly unusual breed which are presented as gun dogs while another is a gun dog kennel producing one of the more commonly seen hunting breeds. You might inquire at both places. The kennel with the unusual breed of *show quality* dogs might charge more for a pup than the gun dog kennel. Which is the better dog? You would be wise to select the gun dog. *Show quality* dogs of hunting breeds are for shows. Gun dogs are for the field. Show dogs sometimes make satisfactory gun dogs, but many times they don't. You must exercise discretion.

Don't shy away from buying a dog sight-unseen. If the breeder is willing to ship you a dog via air-freight, he's probably concerned that you like the dog since you're trusting his good judgment. Call various kennels. Talk to the owners and trainers. Ask them for information. If you have a positive gut-feeling, you'll probably get a quality dog. It's better to place the burden for your satisfaction on a distant kennel with a good reputation to preserve than to allow an unscrupulous *fly-by-night* local operator to cheat you. Who you buy your dog from is important. Proceed with caution and proceed with a plan. Take your time. You'll know the right dog when you find him.

Your dog is a reflection of you.

3

Bringing Home A New Puppy

One of the most emotionally significant days in any dog's life is when he leaves his littermates and the familiar surroundings of the breeder's kennel and goes *home* to his new *family*. Suddenly he is singularly important, and he soon learns to bask in the limelight. Where he may have had less attention, now he is praised, played with, and talked to more often. This is living!

It is very important that you give the pup ample handling and affection so he realizes that all these new experiences are to be enjoyed, leaving no time for homesickness. Where he was previously one of a litter, now he is number one, the object of his new owner's attention and affection. Keep the praise and contact going, and he will associate you and his new *family* with pleasure and security. This in turn will make him realize that he is your dog and that you're the master he is going to please.

Photo 7 by: Rapheal Lieto.

Mike Jenkins with Charlen's Thoropabst. English setters, like most sporting dogs, make excellent family companions.

The first night with his new family is also important since he will have to learn his place in the family structure. If you kennel him outside, make sure his quarters are comfortable by providing a house with clean bedding such as straw, wood shavings, or an old rug. Of course, he should also have a bowl of clean water and food, preferably of the kind he is accustomed to eating.

You might want to provide him with a toy such as a raw-hide bone; having something entertaining to do will make his new facilities seem less boring. Since he won't have his littermates for security and recreation, you might place an old stuffed animal inside his house. Make sure there are no sewed on eyes or other attachments. For the first couple of nights he will feel like he has a buddy and settle down to sleep. Should he bark and whine, however, don't run out and baby him. If you do, he will do it again since the distraction he caused will have achieved the desired result. Your pup must learn that play time is for play, work time is for work, and bed time is for bed. Instilling this idea early will facilitate all future training. While you will make your pup learn to accept his kenneling easily, you'll also make him feel that he hasn't been abandoned. Go visit him frequently, but not when he creates a disturbance; you don't want him to learn that he gets your attention on demand by obnoxious conduct.

There's an old idea still rampant that a house dog is not a good hunting dog. Nothing could be further from the truth. The sporting breeds thrive on approval. The closer they are to you, the more they will do to gain further approval. They love to please; in fact, they live for it. If you make your puppy one of the family and want to have a very close association with him, go ahead and make him a house dog. The company of a well-behaved, completely civilized dog will bring you much pleasure and simplify all training.

Photo 8 by: Christine Tabone.
Chestnut Ridge Night Hawk owned by Christine Tabone of Lincoln Park, Michigan shows his stuff at an early age. There's no doubt this young Brittany likes to point!

The way you introduce your pup (or older dog) to the house is important. Since your home is probably your most valuable possession, your dog is going to have to respect your property and learn to behave as you wish if he is going to live inside with you. There is no need for his soiling your home, chewing objects other than his toys, general mischief, jumping on you, sleeping on the furniture, begging at the table, tearing up garbage, scratching on surfaces, etc. He must be taught acceptable behavior right from the start. Otherwise, he could cost you a lot of money in damage and make himself the object of your contempt instead of affection. Don't tolerate misconduct by excusing it or making it enticing to the pup. When reprimand is necessary, use it. Knowing how you want your dog to behave is important so you and he should have an understanding right from the start. Since he has a little puppy mind and you have an intelligent human mind, you're going to have to communicate to him what it means to become a house dweller with you.

One important thing for you to do is teach your pup where he is to sleep. He shouldn't be able to go wherever he pleases. His place should be in a comfortable wire or plastic airline crate which is large enough for an adult dog of his breed to turn around in, stand up, and stretch. A nice soft blanket will make it a secure, cozy place. This crate should be located close to the family in a room where he sees people and where he is accessible for their lavish affection. The crate itself will afford security and comfort since it is den-like. In order to get your pup accustomed to his *den*, place his food there to get him used to going in. Also, give him treats by placing them inside the crate. When he goes in, try to remember to say *"kennel"* often so that your pup begins learning that the sound *kennel* means *go inside the crate*.

Now that your pup can go inside the crate and find that it is enjoyable, he won't associate it with punishment or deprivation of contact with people. This den-like crate should be his place to sleep at night--every night. Let him spend his first night there. Make sure that you play with him prior to putting him to bed. Don't feed him just before you want him to go to sleep. Be sure to take him outside to relieve himself, always saying *"outside"* so he begins to learn that he is to go out for this purpose.

When you bring him in, gently push him inside the crate. Don't ever give up if he balks. Make sure he has a toy inside. For the first couple of nights, it might be wise to have a teddy bear or some other safe stuffed animal to be his *buddy*. That way he won't feel lonesome. If your puppy cries to get out, ignore him. After he's quiet you might want to go over to him for a little play but only if you initiate the activity. Never allow your pup to demand something of you before he stops objec-

tionable, un-
desirable be-
havior. Before
long your pup will
sleep all night in
the comfort and
security of his
crate, knowing
you're always
around. He's
been taught that
the crate is his
den, a proper
place for him to
spend the night or
other designated
times as well.

The crate is an
excellent tool for
housebreaking.
Pups do not want
to foul the place
where they sleep.

Photo 9 by: Terry Krueger.
Lady's Main Man (Hunter) handles easily for Anne
Jenkins. If you and your dog like each other,
ownership of the dog will be a pleasure.

Knowing this, you can place the pup inside for short times and
then immediately play with him and then say "*outside*." Then
it's out the door for him to find that perfect spot. When he's
done, bring him back in. Try to make sure he never has an
accident in the house. Knowing the procedure for relieving
himself, your pup will soon be going to the door when he needs
to go. Remember that dogs learn what they do. If you make
him go outside for the excretory function and establish the
right pattern, that's the way it is going to be always. If you're
not vigilant, however, there might be an accident. To prevent

this, don't leave your pup unattended. If no one can remain in the house with him, put him in his kennel. Of course, make sure that you have withheld his food and water for a while and that you've first allowed him to go *outside*.

If you acquired your pup in the dead of winter and if he's not acclimated to cold weather, you'll have to modify the training to include paper training instead of going directly outside. This is worth the effort but start getting him acclimated as soon as possible with short trips *outside* during the warmest, sunniest time of the day.

Let your pup know his bounds. If there are certain rooms where you don't want him, simply do not allow him there. If you don't want him on the furniture, don't hold him in your lap while sitting on the sofa. If you don't want him to jump, push him down when he jumps on you and he'll soon get the picture. During your meal time you should put your puppy in his kennel, saying *"kennel."* Then have your meal. Never feed him from the table by throwing him table scraps. If you encourage him to watch you eat, he'll soon be begging at the table. By the same token, don't give him food such as meat trimmings when you're cooking. Your pup has to learn that he only gets food during designated meal times. Place his food and water before him and let him eat and drink. If he's not interested, remove the food and water. Never feed a young pup *free choice* if he's a house dog. Pups are stimulated to relieve themselves after eating and drinking. Remember that the key to effective house training is to prevent accidents (even one), establishing through repetition the only acceptable pattern.

No is a very important word for your puppy to know. It means *stop what you're doing - now!* Every time your young pup does something which is against the rules you want him to abide by, you must force him to stop by commanding *"no!"*

Before long he will desist from jumping on you, sitting on the furniture, begging at the table, entering off-limits areas, and chewing on unauthorized objects. The key to developing a civilized house dog is consistency regarding permissible actions. Never condone an infringement one time yet punish it another. That which is forbidden is forbidden always.

Once your pup understands what you expect of him in the house or kennel, he'll be a pleasure to own. Always let him know what's allowed and what isn't. By teaching him the meaning of *no*, you'll be able to curb a lot of other undesirable behavior like nuisance barking, digging holes in your yard, tearing up property, rummaging through garbage, chasing cars, joggers, or bicyclists, attacking cats, etc. If your dog knows the limits, he will comply with your wishes, thereby assuring a special place with you in which he remains in your good graces.

> *Through hard work, you can have it all -- the point, the handling, the retrieve, etc. You can have a finished gun dog if you want one.*

4

The Breeds

There are many breeds of dogs developed for hunting, and there are good and poor individuals in every breed. Some of these individuals may have inherent strengths

Photo 10 by Len Jenkins.
Charlen's Bill Crockett, a hard-working English setter, pointing a covey of quail at the writer's training grounds in Monroe County, Michigan.

and weaknesses; and all are affected one way or another by environment, human interaction, and general experience.

The key to developing your own gun dog lies first in selecting a young, unspoiled prospect from a good breeding program in which the breeder selected for what you consider desirable traits. This breeding program should stress general soundness, stamina, intelligence, calmness, nose, desire to hunt, and sound personalities free of meanness, nervousness, timidity, cowardice, or sluggishness. It takes a lot of heart and mind to make a bird dog; and if the breeding program only stressed cosmetics, you will have a handicap you may never overcome.

Also, don't complicate matters by opting for some unusual *off the wall* breed about which you have just heard. Oftentimes these highly-touted, unusual breeds are nothing more

Photo 11 by Christine Tabone.

Chestnut Ridge Rocky Rambo (JH, CH) is a superb Brittany spaniel owned by Christine Tabone of Lincoln Park, Michigan. Rambo is trained to perfection and functions as both a practical upland gun dog as well as an outstanding field trial contender.

than a mystique and great expense. The best gun dogs in the world for North American game and North American conditions are right here. These dogs were developed for what we hunt; if the breeding program from which they came followed basic Darwinian principles, the unfit were weeded out long ago, not exported.

Photo 12 by Dick Geswein. A German shorthaired pointer on point in Waterloo, Ohio.

If you are a pointing dog enthusiast, consider the setter (English) and pointer. These should be your first choice if you are looking for a superb field dog with high style. Of course, your choice should also involve consideration of the dog's background. Is it of field or show breeding? Although there are American Kennel Club (AKC) or dual-registered individuals, a setter or pointer registered with Field Dog Stud Book (FDSB) is probably your best bet.

Should you like other pointing breeds, however, there are some excellent Brittany spaniels and German shorthaired pointers. These dogs can be very stylish, and they compare favorably with the setters and pointers. Many have an excellent nose and look good in every respect despite the short tail. If you like Britts or shorthairs, look to a kennel specializing in gun dogs, not show dogs. You should be aware that Brittany spaniels and German short-haired pointers are usually registered with the AKC. Many breeders special-ize in either field or bench-type dogs. As a sportsman, you'll be interested in a dog from fine AKC field breeding.

Photo 13 by Len Jenkins.
Bob Andre of Troy, Michigan training his young Gordon setter, Carly, at the writer's training grounds in Monroe County, Michigan.

While the other setters, the Gordon and Irish, are beautiful, you might have a problem finding a good one. The problem itself is the dog's beauty. It seems the people who are excessively *hung up* over conformation and show standards, to the exclusion of other traits, have almost engineered a freak. These dogs may be considered beautiful while standing still, but they are a far cry from the superb gun dogs they once were. This is man's fault--not the dog's. If you can identify a fine field bred Gordon or Irish setter selected from hunting stock, go for it. If not, stick with the basics--your setter, pointer, Britt or German shorthaired pointer.

If you don't mind missing points and don't care much for pointing dogs generally, consider the retrieving and flushing breeds. The Labrador retriever, Golden retriever,

Chesapeake Bay retriever and springer spaniel from a field-bred background could provide you with plenty of fast action and excitement. While other breeds could be used as well, these two seem to account for the majority of fine-quality upland flush dogs. The cocker spaniel or the other retriever breeds might catch your fancy, but just be sure it is what you want and that you have researched the particular dog's hunting background.

If you wish to start with one of the versatile breeds, Brittany spaniels and German shorthaired pointers are generally standouts. There are also others, notably the vizsla, Weimaraner, griffon, German wirehaired pointer, and pudelpointer, although they are not frequently seen. There just might be a special individual in one of these breeds for you. While the versatile or Continental breeds are promoted as

Photo 14 by John Laney.
Molly, a merry little springer spaniel, works hard for owners John Laney and son, John, of Newport, Michigan. A springer is a flushing dog which can be used for hunting both game birds and rabbits. Molly never quits!

Photo 15 by Cyril Keiffer.
Scout, a fun-loving Golden retriever, co-owned by Cyril Keiffer of Temperance, Michigan and John Erkert of Toledo, Ohio, excels as both a companion and a field dog.

Jacks-of-all-trades, you might be better off sticking with a specialist. The odds are in your favor that you will be most satisfied with a stylish pointer or setter for upland gunning, a hard-going Lab for waterfowl hunted in ice-cold waters, and of course, a beagle for rabbits. Just because a breed is promoted as being adept at all tasks doesn't mean it's as accomplished as a specialist in each field. Should you seek out one of the rare, more exotic breeds for romantic or sentimental reasons, be sure to inquire if the breeder put hunting performance first and foremost in his breeding program.

While there are fine individuals in all the recognized sporting breeds, there are good reasons for the popularity of certain breeds and the lack of interest in others.

Photo 16 by Dan Wizner.

Zack, a young Chesapeake Bay retriever, owned by Tom and Vivian DeRiemaker of Detroit, Michigan, is attracted to this Midland County marsh. Zack is being trained as both an upland flushing dog and waterfowl retriever.

*Start with a pup, not an older dog.
There's no short cut!*

5

You And Your Pup:
How About A Partnership?

So, you've brought home a puppy! Assuming that your pup comes from strong, healthy stock developed for grouse hunting, you have made a wise selection. The pup should have strong hunting desire and pointing instinct bred into him and, with your nurturing and training, this pup just might realize his potential. Just might--provided you do the right things at the right time. And the right time is probably **now**.

All too often sportsmen acquire otherwise excellent pups which somehow don't quite measure up to what most would consider excellence in the grouse woods. Many of these pups become pretty good gun dogs in spite of their owner's unintentional oversights. Yet, maximum potential is not fully realized, and the hunter's maximum satisfaction is not realized because he's overlooked the importance of *pre-school*. That's early training in which the pup learns basic commands, cooperative activity, respect, love, restraint and, above all, the ability to be at ease with himself. There are a few premises that you as the pup's owner must accept in order to make *pre-school* effective:

The young pup is vulnerable and weak.

If you deliberately or inadvertantly terrorize the pup using excessive force, surprise, or loudness, he will cower. This manner is in itself disgusting and does not speak well for either dog or master. It is a learned response and becomes part

Photo 17 by: Bill Bolyard.
This classy eight-week old setter loves to point. All she needs from her owner is encouragement and guidance to develop her inherent abilities.

of your dog's character if done too often. Therefore, in your training, be firm and loving and consistent. Don't cower your dog! If you do, he may forever display a cowering manner at the slightest provocation.

Dogs are dependent animals.

They require approval for mental well-being. They do not like confrontation. A dog thrives on attention to his needs and loves petting. Consoling, supportive, enthusiastic talk gives him great pleasure while verbal abuse causes insecurity and fright. The more he thinks you love him, the more he will do for you. A grouse dog in particular must have a positive relationship with the hunter. After all, he is hunting for two reasons: he loves the sport and it pleases you. If he does not care about you, he could turn into a self-hunter. And you could turn to force. The end result would be a miserable grouse hunt for both hunter and dog.

Dogs learn through repetition.

Decide what you want to teach your dog and begin early. If your pup is six to eight weeks old, this is the time to start. Although these early sessions are fun for both dog and owner, nonetheless, they are still training sessions. In fact, everything you do with your dog is *training*. Consistency on your part is a must!

So, what should a grouse dog pup of six weeks be taught? There are just a few basics. For instance, teach your dog his name. Say it often. From there you should teach him to come to you by using the word *come* and one whistle blast. Always use the same signal! Each time you call him, do it the same way, repeating the command as needed in an enthusiastic tone.

Next, teach him to move forward on your frequent forays together into the field. Do this with two whistle blasts. Start with the pup when he is very young and short-legged. It is a great way to develop a close-working gun dog.

As you walk with your dog, zigzag. Don't go in a straight line. Each time you change direction, give two whistle blasts and an exaggerated arm signal. Do it the same way each time, and soon your pup will quarter and move forward with enthusiasm. A good pup will probably sight-point a wing on a rod. When working with the wing, teach **whoa**. That is **w-h-o-a**... But discontinue the wing and rod as soon as **whoa** is learned because you ultimately want your pup to point scent, not sight.

Leash-break your puppy, but don't use force. Don't scare him; it isn't necessary. If he resists the leash, let him romp around trailing the leash behind him. Before long, he won't mind it. Your pup should be taught to **heel**, but it is not necessary to have him **sit**. Save **sit** for later. After all, you want your pup to point with high head and tail in a proud manner. There is no sense in teaching him that **sit** is a virtue because he may start to sit or crouch too low on point. Sometimes signals get mixed!

All of your interaction with your pup should be positive. Before long, your pup will know his name, **come** when called, know two whistle signals and a hand signal, hold a point on **whoa**, quarter at fairly close range, walk on a lead, **heel**, enjoy going afield with you, and respond to your enthusiasm.

Yet there will be times when he will test your dominance over him and perhaps strain your friendship. At such times he should be constructively punished, provided he knows what he did wrong and that he flagrantly disobeyed your command. At such times he should be punished by harsh words, ordered **no** and perhaps physically reprimanded with a light cuff. Because his relationship with you has already been established through the bonds developed through *pre-school* training, he will be so jolted by your displeasure that he will not easily risk incurring your wrath in the future. From this point on, the temporary loss of your affection will be sufficient to keep your dog in line. Your dog is now ready for *advanced* training.

A good grouse dog must love both his sport and his master. Such a dog is a pleasure to hunt over because he can be easily controlled in the woods. Because the bond between him and his master has been well established, particularly during those crucial early weeks of *pre-school*, he will check back willingly and frequently while you trust his nose and follow him through the woods.

You and he are indeed a team. There is no need for aggression, yelling or scolding after your dog has been effectively trained. You and he can both fully enjoy the sport of grouse hunting, ending each hunt refreshed and renewed.

Your dog is not a machine. You must work with him yourself, even if you've had him trained for you.

6

A Dog's Limited
Working Vocabulary

Dogs *read* their owners and handlers in a variety of ways. While body language, eye contact, and tone of voice convey certain messages to the dog, the most important and useful messages are communicated in a few short words which the dog learns through training.

While a variety of sounds and signals can be taught to the dog, the following words are useful, and every upland gun dog should know their meaning:

Come

- This means *get over here now!* You may wish to use a variant form such as *come here* or simply *here*. Whatever word you choose, however, use it the

same way and in the same form each time you give
this command.

Heel

- This means *walk quietly on the handler's left side.*
The dog must not pull on the lead, dart to the side
or hang back, whether on the lead or not. He must
coordinate his pace with that of the handler.

Whoa

- This means *stop moving right now!* If the dog was
on point, the word *whoa* means that he must hold
his point with full style. If he was instructed to *whoa*
while heeling or told to *whoa* in his location (stop
and stay), he must remain there without moving.

No!

- This means s*top what you are doing now!* This
command must always be given in a demanding,
authoritative, loud voice so the dog understands
that he must *cease and desist.*

Fetch

- This means *go get a thrown object and retrieve it to
hand.* This also means find and retrieve a downed
bird when the command is given in conjunction
with *Dead.*

Dead

- This is the only command on which a dog is
permitted to take the bird into his mouth. Fetch is

used in association with this command. It means
find and retrieve the downed bird.

Bird

- This command or a variant of it like *find the bird*
  means that the dog is to *actively pursue and search
  for birds*. It is a useful word for getting the dog out
  in front and signals the beginning of the hunt.
  Initially it should be used only when the trainer
  knows birds are present and can be located.

Give

- This means *relinquish the bird* after the retrieve by
  dropping it into the handler's hand.

Kennel

- This means *hop into the pen, shipping crate, or
  vehicle* eagerly when told to do so. Knowing this
  term is useful as it minimizes inconvenience at the
  end of the hunt because the dog will go directly to
  his place when commanded to do so. No chasing,
  catching, or cajoling is necessary.

The dog also responds to other signals and sounds. The
whistle signal (single or multiple toots given consistently) is
the dog's cue to execute a certain task or behavior. The
whistle signal should ideally be given in conjunction with a
hand signal. For instance, waving the arm forward or lowering
the arm briskly by slapping your thigh can signal to the dog
that he should go forward and/or change direction and come
in on command, respectively.

Each word or signal is to have a single meaning in order
to avoid confusion. For instance, you can teach your dog to

Photo 18 by Len Jenkins.

Nice enough for a lady. A well disciplined dog is a joy for the entire family. Bill always behaves in a civilized manner for Anne, Danielle and Elizabeth.

come in on *Come*. You would confuse him unnecessarily if you say *"Come On"* or a variant form when you wish for him to move out <u>away</u> from you. Instead of *Come On* you could substitute phrases like *Let's Go, Find The Bird*, or some other phrase of your choosing. *Come* only means *come in to me <u>now</u>!* It only means <u>one</u> thing.

In teaching the various words, it is important that you say each word distinctly and clearly. Don't intermix the words or use them in context other than what your dog was taught. Repetition and praise are essential in teaching these words. Once your dog understands their meaning and chooses not to comply with the directive, reprimand is in order. When giving a command, be sure to maintain as much eye contact with the dog as possible so that he knows you are concentrating on him. A command is a command, not a request. You're not negotiating. Say what you mean and follow through, but avoid talking too much so that your dog doesn't learn that he does not have to comply until after several identical commanding words or signals are given. A command always means *Comply Now!*

Dogs learn what they do. If they do it right, they learn it right. If they do it wrong, they learn it wrong.

7

Gun Dog Jargon

Like others who participate in a specialized activity, upland gun dog enthusiasts have their own jargon. The following is part of that jargon:

Back Casting

- While a dog usually searches for game in front of the hunter, a back casting dog searches behind. Sometimes a dog will work in front nicely and then cast back, coming up from behind the hunter. Although game is sometimes found behind, it's best to discourage back casting.

Backing

- This is the same as *honoring*. A dog backs when he points another dog which is pointing game. If you hunt with another hunter who has a dog, make sure your dog backs (or honors). Nobody likes a dog who steals points.

Blinking

- This is a heavy-duty fault in a bird dog! A blinking dog avoids game which he knows is present or refuses to hunt further. A blinker, or bird-shy dog, may never be completely cured. Such a dog has had a bad experience with a bird. Perhaps he was spurred by one or in some way reprimanded by the handler using a bird to strike the dog. Bird-shyness is caused. Be careful. This is a serious, hard-to-correct fault. Don't make a problem.

Bolting

- This could ruin a hunt big time! A bolting dog runs off to self-hunt and ignores his handler.

Bumping

- If a dog either crowds his birds or inadvertently runs into them causing a flush, he's bumping his birds. If yours is a flush dog, bumping shouldn't bother you too much. However, if yours is a pointing dog, you've got a problem. This is a correctable problem which must be addressed.

Cast

- This is the distance a dog extends while hunting. He could either cast forward and then work back or *quarter*, casting side to side in front of the gunner

while moving forward, sweeping a field in windshield wiper fashion.

Cover

- Always pick good cover for your hunts. This refers to sufficient vegetation to provide habitat for game birds.

Covert

- This term usually refers to the cover in which one would find grouse. It's mostly heavy vegetation--thickets, woodlots, brush, and abandoned grown-up orchards.

Covey

- This is a group of birds, usually quail.

Covey Rise

- This is an exciting sight to behold. A large group of birds, usually quail, rise up in flight together. It gets the adrenalin pumping!

Flagging

- This refers to a dog's being soft on point because of uncertainty or indecision. He wags or flags the tail rather rigidly while on point. It's not very pretty yet some dogs seem to flag even when on a solid point. If you like your dog's overall performance, you may wish to overlook the flagging.

Forced Retrieving

- If a dog does not retrieve naturally, he can be forced to do so on command by using forced retrieving techniques. In forced retrieving, the handler applies pressure to the dog's ear while commanding *"Fetch."* When the command has been executed, the pressure is relieved.

Gun-Shy

- A dog who is afraid of the gun report is gun shy. Such a dog may cower down and tremble or run off to the vehicle or to some distant place to hide. It's best to prevent gun-shyness through proper introduction to the gun. Although this is a serious problem, it can be cured.

Honoring

- See backing.

Hard Mouth

- If a dog savagely attacks the downed bird by tearing it up, he has a hard mouth. This is a serious fault, but it can be corrected.

Hup

- This is a command used by spaniel trainers to make their dog sit or stop on the command "*Hup*." Compliance with this command ensures that the dog will not be in the line of fire as the quarry is flushed.

Making Game

- This refers to the excitement dogs show when game is near. There is a marked increase in enthusiasm with cracking merry tail and perky facial and ear expression. The dog's body language shouts "I'm excited!"

Man Shy

- If a dog is anti-social and avoids contact with humans, he's man shy. Most gun dogs are very social. A man shy dog was probably made that way by abusive handling.

Marking

- A dog will mark the point where game falls after it is shot. He will then go directly to that location for the retrieve.

Pointing Dead

- This occurs when the dog finds a downed dead or crippled bird and goes on point rather than making the retrieve. It's not a terribly undesirable trait because the dog at least locates the downed game. With work, such a dog can be taught to retrieve.

Quartering

- Casting from side to side within a reasonable range while moving forward in front of the gunner is desirable because a good swath can be worked. While doing so the dog maintains an energetic pace and merry tail. This ground covering pattern is known as quartering. This is frequently a natural trait in bird dogs although it usually has to be developed through training.

Scent Pointing

- A good bird dog uses his nose, not his eyes, as a stimulus for the point. If he goes on point when he smells birds, he is scent pointing. This is what you want!

Self Hunting

- A self-hunter is a bolting dog. Such a dog does not care to have the hunter around because he's in the habit of experiencing plenty of action his way. Prevent your dog from becoming a self-hunter by preventing him from running away from you. Create a dependence by making the dog realize that he needs you for his sport. This can be done by lots of training in which many birds are shot over the dog. Make your dog need you!

Sight Pointing

- A dog sight points when he relies on visual rather than olfactory stimuli. Excessive rewards for sight pointing a wing on a fishing rod will lead to over-dependence on the eyes if done for too long a period. Let your dog sight point only long enough to learn *whoa*.

Style

- A dog with style is one which is agile, animated, and athletic. A stylish gun dog carries a high head and a high tail.

Style Up

- When a bird dog is on point, he can be styled up by the handler. In styling up, the dog's tail and stance are adjusted to improve his appearance on point. A high tail is preferred.

Trailing

- A dog which does not actively hunt on his own but merely follows another dog is trailing. If a dog is a follower, do not run him with another dog. If you go out in the field with such a dog and he trails you, it's likely that your dog lacks desire for the hunt. If you can't figure out a way to get the dog working, you may want to start over with a more willing prospect.

Whoa

- This command means *stop now*. A whoa stake is used to *whoa* train. All bird dogs must *whoa*.

Wild Flush

- Birds which flush ahead of the dog but are not bumped by the dog constitute a wild flush. It's not the dog's fault. The birds are simply spooky and flush wildly far ahead of the dog.

Winding

- This refers to the dog's keeping his head up and seeking scent. The nostrils are used to sift scents and the dog proceeds in the direction of the scent.

Yard Training

- The discipline involved in teaching a dog to *heel, come, whoa, stay, fetch,* etc. is yard training. Yard train your dog prior to field training him.

For success you must hold high expectations of yourself as well as your dog.

8

Predictability

The typical well-bred bird dog is what he is because of a combination of factors. First of all, he either *has it* or he doesn't as far as nose, instinct, and desire to please are concerned. No matter how hard you try, you'll never make him point a bird if he doesn't have the nose. Similarly, he won't work with style and enthusiasm if he doesn't like either the sport or you. There have to be some *givens* to make your efforts pay off. If your dogs lacks the nose, the heart, the brains, and the desire, you would be better off to start with a new prospect and relegate your dog to some other calling in life.

Although the dog must have raw talent if he's to amount to much, you must also do your part if his potential for performance is to be realized. You're the trainer, the one with the intellect as well as the power. Whether your dog achieves as well as you expect has much to do with how you develop his

abilities. To simply throw your arms up in despair without first evaluating your efforts and techniques is to waste much potential. To place the blame on the animal and not the master, the one with reasoning power, is a cop-out. If you train *smart*, you'll get a lot out of a good prospect.

Think before you act. What is it you want from your dog? How will you be able to get it from him? Pattern is very important as you train. If you do things in a predictable way and set up situations in which your dog works in a desired manner, you're on your way. Be a *set up artist* of sorts. If you set up circumstances in which your dog does what you want and does it well, this pattern will be learned. If you train so that he performs a task incorrectly, he will learn it this way. Let him learn from his mistakes whenever possible, but don't let him continue making those mistakes because he'll simply learn to continue that pattern, not the desired one.

Let's say you've thought things out. You have a good base from which to work in that your dog knows certain words and has had enough yard training to make him a civilized partner in the field. Let's say that he likes you. Let's go one step further. Let's say he also respects you and knows where you stand regarding his conduct. Such a dog can achieve because he enjoys a good rapport with his owner and also feels the security of knowing bounds and requirements. For him, there's a lot at stake. He won't risk losing your approval and the security of knowing what's acceptable and what isn't.

If your dog loves and respects you, you've got a fine foundation from which to work. However, in order to preserve this foundation, you have to continue thinking ahead of your dog by preparing a response to his performance and behavior. Because reward is tremendously important, don't overlook its value. When your dog does things well, reward and praise him lavishly. Do this each time during early training. Even well into your work with him, let him feel your approval. It will give him the motivation to continue. Your satisfaction is too important to his sense of self-worth. He's going to work to preserve this positive relationship as he knows it from your reward and approval.

While praise for the positive is an essential training technique, punishment, a meaningful consequence for disobedience and misconduct, is also important and must be sure and swift when needed. It must, like praise, be predictable. Of course, the type of punishment must match the severity of the offense and be intelligently administered. This punishment can take the form of a harsh word, a physical reprimand, or a withholding of affection. It depends on many factors, including the dog's temperament. In no case, however, should misconduct or disobedience go unpunished. While punishment is a good technique for curbing misconduct, it should be administered in a reasoned, constructive manner, never emotionally or angrily.

Hopefully, your dog was taught *No*. This command means *stop what you're doing--now!* If he doesn't know the meaning of *No*, you had better teach him real soon. Understanding *No* could keep him out of trouble and could even save his life. It will also facilitate further training.

Don't give a command unless you are able to enforce it. You must be able to punish him if your dog flagrantly disregards your command. Your dog must know that he has to comply. He's not your equal and you're not negotiating with him. You're giving an order, not making a request. He must understand that you mean what you say and that disregarding your command will most definitely result in unpleasant consequences. If you can't enforce your command, don't give it! At least that way you'll only have a performance problem to correct. You don't ever want your dog to think he can ignore your commands.

A dog that knows where both he and you stand is a happy, secure dog. You're not doing your dog a favor if you indulge him to excess. He has to know that your approval and love are too important to lose. If your dog perceives you as being sloppy in your expectations, he won't respect you. For maximum performance, he must not think of you as being a *wimp*. He must know you mean and do what you say, predictably-- every time, with no exceptions. There's security in knowing this, and this security is necessary to your dog's emotional well-being. If you want a happy, secure, self-confident dog, be predictable.

Because they love to please by nature, dogs are quite easily trained. They thrive on your approval and have tremendous potential for preserving and nurturing your approval by doing very sophisticated, intricate work in the field. This desire to please and to love and to be loved in return can only be preserved satisfactorily if you are predictable in your requirements and expectations. If you do things in a predictable manner, demand crisp execution of commands, reward and punish, and take advantage of your dog's need for your approval, your dog will perform well for you and meet your expectations. If you expect a lot from him, you'll get it. If you expect little, you'll get even less.

You must be a set-up artist, setting your dog up for success through structured training which simulates the demands of actual hunting.

9

Consistency

Was Machiavelli right when he said that it is better to be feared than loved? Think about that assertion in terms of your dog. Surely you want your dog to love you since it is in the nature of sporting dogs to want to please. They will work their hearts out for you just for your approval. But what if they have nothing to fear when they run out into a road, chase deer, break point prematurely, refuse to come when called, or disobey whistle or hand signals? Such flagrant disregard for doing the right thing could be more than a source of embarrassment. It could lead to the dog's jeopardizing his own life and safety. A disobedient dog detracts from the hunt. He causes tension and contempt to mar what otherwise should constitute a rewarding and relaxing experience. If your dog has no fear of you when he ignores your commands, he will cheat both you and himself out of the full enjoyment of the hunt.

So, was Machiavelli right? Yes and no with regard to canines. You must be both feared and loved. In the case of human/ canine dynamics, there must be kindness and affection. The dog needs your approval for his psychological well-being. By the same token, if you don't like your dog, he will sense your feelings and never work to his full potential because of his own uncertainty and distrust. You must both feel at ease with one another and have a sense of trust. Anytime your dog blatantly disobeys what he knows is one of your rules, he should expect and get the force of your displeasure.

Discipline should take the form of a verbal reprimand, a shaking by the collar, or a light cuff. But regardless of what form the punishment takes, it must be matched to the dog's ability to tolerate punishment. With some dogs, a harsh word is sufficient

Photo 19 by: Brad Belanger.
Thoropabst Lew rests after a successful hunt in Michigan. Brad Belanger acquired Lew as a puppy and developed him into a finished gun dog himself!

while others require more stringent measures if they are to respect your wishes and learn to modify their behavior in the future. In no case, however, should obvious disobedience be tolerated. The problem will only get worse and the dog's life will necessarily worsen as he misbehaves. He won't be able to enjoy the full value of your admiration and affection for him. Your failure to correct will only confuse him. Therefore, if you love your dog, teach him respect for you by making the punishment immediate and predictable when he violates the code of behavior you expect him to follow.

To excuse misconduct sometimes and punish it at others is inconsistent indeed. Dogs are highly intuitive creatures who need to know limits. Be kind to your dog but discipline him when necessary to make sure he always understands those limits. Your consistent, persistent, and insistent response to any recalcitrance will guarantee a happy and productive long-term relationship with your gun dog.

> *Your dog always knows when you're not paying attention to him. He'll take advantage of it too!*

10

Needed:
The Right Attitude

If you want to train your dog successfully, you will have to approach your task with the right attitude. In fact, a prerequisite to accomplishment in any endeavor is a constructive attitude in which you systematically work toward your goal. Without a constructive attitude, you're doomed to failure.

Any person with reasonably good judgment can train a bird dog. However, if you aren't motivated by the desire to own a classy, well-trained gun dog, your effort might be in vain. If you want success, you'll have it, provided you think positively, have faith in your dog, and maintain confidence in yourself.

Positive thinking will serve you well. Anything is possible if enough effort and planning go into it. Dog training is no exception. There is no place in the process for doubt, anger, or defeatism. These are negative forces which will sap your energy and motivation and lead to dismal failure. Although slow progress can lead to doubt and disappointment, don't dwell on negative factors. Instead, proceed with your mission by always being patient with your dog, consistent in your training strategy, and supportive of your dog by rewarding and recognizing improvement.

Photo 20 by: Darla Naylor.

This Utah ringneck doesn't stand a chance! A trio of setters owned by Bob Naylor of Wellington, Utah has the bird nailed down with no place to run.

Have faith in your dog. He'll learn if you think he will. If you expect him to be a finished gun dog, that's what he will be. If you think he's a loser, he'll be that. You get what you expect. If you expect a lot from him and preserve your faith in his ability to master the various tasks you are teaching him, he will be a gun dog you'll be proud to own. Having faith in your dog will build his confidence. This in turn will lead to an improvement in his animation and enthusiasm, bringing you much personal satisfaction in the field.

While having faith in your dog is crucial to success, you must also have faith in yourself. If you're a patient, determined individual who can analyze a task and then devise a strategy for its execution, you can train your own dog. With self-confidence you can develop his bird-finding and bird-handling abilities one step at a time until you get the finished product. If you decide, however, that you're not satisfied with the progress, scale down your expectations for each step or change your techniques. What may work with one dog may not work for another. Only you can determine what needs to be done. You'll still get the desired result although you may have to change your approach. Analyze what needs to be done and devise the right strategy for accomplishing your objective through short and long-term goal setting and improved time management techniques. Success is in reach.

While money can buy you the services of an excellent gun dog trainer, you can also train your own dog, saving the money and gaining satisfaction. Positive thinking is crucial. By maintaining faith in both yourself and your dog, you will have the kind of gun dog that will bring a new dimension to your hunting experience. Go ahead now; you can do it!

You get what you expect. If you expect a lot, you get a lot. If you expect little, you get even less!

11

Realistic Goal Setting

If you want a well-trained gun dog that handles easily, finds birds, points with style, and retrieves to hand, you can have it if you want it seriously enough. In fact, if the prospect you are training has the ability and if you make the commitment, you'll have a finished gun dog of which you can be proud. However, you can only work toward this objective one step at a time. You have to plan out a strategy that will work effectively, setting short and long term goals for which you structure the nature and the sequence of training. Don't expect a finished wonder dog over night! It takes time for training and time for the dog to absorb what you are trying to teach him. By setting realistic goals over a sufficient period of time, you will accomplish a great deal provided you plan your work, proceed one step at a time in order to build to the desired result, and constantly review and reinforce what's already been learned.

Like a teacher, you have to plan your work and then work your plan. Before you even start, decide on your mission in terms of both the immediate and long range changes you want to see in the dog. When you decide what you want to do, start training and guide your dog along until you achieve the desired results. It is your game plan, not the dog's. He will learn happily and willingly if you execute your plan in a logical manner.

In order to train your dog effectively, you have to proceed one step at a time, realizing that each phase of the training process leads to the finished product, a composite of many small efforts. It requires a great deal of learning and coordination with his owner's wishes for a dog to become a finished gun dog. If you analyze the training process and proceed systematically, you'll make significant progress. In doing so, it is vital that you keep your sessions up-beat and short. Many short pleasant lessons are superior to just a few long grueling sessions which might in the long run sour your dog. While the lessons are best short and pleasant, you must insist on mastery along the way. The feeling of accomplishment for both you and the dog will help generate renewed incentive and enthusiasm which will lead to success. If the dog feels he is pleasing you and if you feel you are achieving something, you'll both gain immense satisfaction. This satisfaction is realized in small doses, culminating eventually in a class gun dog that will provide you with many years of pleasure afield.

The training process amounts to a series of lessons which builds up to complete mastery. You can't train your dog to seek game, quarter, obey, point, and retrieve all in one step. You must start with the fundamentals and build from there by putting the various steps together. If you train *smart* and make the dog learn each step and then see how each relates to every other step, you'll have something. Put the steps together and always reward your dog when proper execution of task is achieved. Your dog will enjoy doing the things which he does well so you should continually review learned tasks and reward him constantly. You will also enjoy training more if you remind yourself frequently of your accomplishments as a trainer. If you don't gain satisfaction in this manner, it is unlikely that your dog will.

It will be amazing how rapidly you'll develop a finished gun dog if you train systematically. You might find that the best way to achieve your goals is to write out a schedule and get a clear picture of what you want to accomplish by a particular time. Know your goals. If you don't know what you want, neither will your dog. If you don't analyze the training process and insist on mastery, your dog will flounder. If you don't put the steps together in a logical manner, your dog will never see any relevance to your efforts. And finally, if you don't reward your dog by showing your approval, he won't have the heart to want to please.

Analyze the training process,
teaching one command at a time.

12

Everything Is Training

Through the training and handling you have provided, your dog is a reflection of you. While you will have to schedule time and structure methods in a formal manner in order to properly train your dog, there is still another component to the process. This component, while sometimes overlooked, is always present and crucially important. Everything you do with your dog constitutes training. All interaction is a vital part of the process.

In order to ensure success for you as well as your dog, establish a friendly relationship first. If you don't, you may find that your dog does not want to be around you. This of course will complicate the teaching of *Come Here* and everything else you try to do with your dog when he is not on a lead and under your immediate physical control. Once your dog likes you and wants to be with you, you have it made. Make him want more interaction but start creating bounds--limits to his behavior and actions--which initiate your continued approval if these bounds are honored. If the acceptable bounds are violated, however, your dog will have to learn that your displeasure will follow. In order to resume the comfortable arrangement in which he basks in approval, he will soon learn to avoid the behavior or resistance which triggered the displeasure, correction, or reprimand. His sense of security and need for approval compel him to respect you and to comply with your expectations of him at all times.

Knowing how important it is to make your dog want interaction with you, you can incorporate this factor into your training by intensifying his need for your acceptance and desire to do whatever it takes to keep it. The key is consistency in your treatment of him. If you think about what you are doing, you will accomplish much in the way of training whenever you are simply with your dog. For instance, if your dog runs up to you, praise him lavishly and let him know you are happy to see him. By the same token, if he is in his kennel, go to him and at least talk to him so he knows you want to be with him also. The bonding which occurs will help prevent other problems down the way. Remember, a hunting dog is thrilled to be in the field doing what he instinctively loves doing. If he doesn't really like you or feel that it is important to gain your approval, he will probably remain just out of your range and ignore your calls. Such a situation could have been avoided had you taken full advantage of your dog's need for approval.

While you have to respond positively to the things your dog does to please you, you must also respond to the things which are wrong. The dog doesn't know what is acceptable and what is not unless you teach him. For instance, if he runs up to you and jumps on you, push him back down firmly and then praise him for coming. He is just happy to be with you

Photo 21 by: B. McDermid.
Cinder, owned by the McDermids of Soldotna, Alaska, can't get her mind off that spruce grouse!

and wants to get closer. If the jumping bothers you, let him know and he will stop it as soon as he learns that you like him to run to you but that you do not like the jumping. Always let the dog know that the negative response on your part is a response to the unacceptable conduct, not to the dog himself. In play, your dog may run to you and jump. You may feel in a relaxed mood and figure it is no big deal now because you are not *training*. If that is the case, you are going to confuse your dog with mixed signals, telling him that sometimes it's okay to jump and other times it isn't. He will have to try to figure out which is which. In order to head off a possible problem, you should communicate to your dog that it is never okay to jump on you, whether at play or work. This could easily be taught during your frequent daily interactions your dog.

Everything else you do is also important. Don't give a command and then change your mind about it if the dog doesn't obey. This just teaches him that sometimes it doesn't matter whether he obeys or not. If he does not comply immediately, don't send him the message that he can obey when he gets around to it. If he is way out in the field, don't let him remain there without you. He just might become a self-hunter if he does. If he fails to point, to retrieve, to pick up a bird, to heel, or to whoa, don't excuse it sometimes and get angry about it other times. If your dog chases a bicyclist or motorist, don't punish him in one instance and ignore the infraction in another. If your pup chews up a shoe, don't get angry if it's a new shoe and excuse it if it's old. Your pup can't discriminate new from old. You must teach him that chewing up anything in the house will result in punishment. Think about your messages. If you want your dog to be a class gun dog and respond to your training, you shouldn't confuse him. You will accomplish a great deal in your formal training only if you are consistent in your actions and expectations in all daily interactions. You'll have your dog conditioned to your expectations. This will lead to security and certainty on his part. This will in turn lead to great personal satisfaction for you, a tremendous reward for your clear, definite, unconditional signals in all your dog's experiences with you.

All dogs, like humans, can be better!

13

Thirty Training Thoughts Worth Remembering

Excuses abound so it is very easy to find one for every-thing. The nice thing about excuses is that they pro-vide an escape for the dog owner who finds it difficult to take responsibility for what his gun dog has become. Rather than make excuses for the things beyond your control, evaluate your input to the total training process. The following thirty training thoughts should be considered periodically while working with your dog.

- You get what you expect. If you expect a lot, you get a lot. If you expect little, you get even less.
- All interaction with your dog is training.
- Dogs learn what they do. If they do it right, they learn it right. If they do it wrong, they learn it wrong.

- Training is like a jigsaw puzzle. You complete the puzzle one piece at a time.

- There is no progress without incentive.

- If you want an excuse, you'll find one.

- For success, you must hold high expectations of yourself as well as your dog.

- Your dog is a reflection of you.

- Never allow your dog unconditional freedom to run through the field as he chooses. He must learn that he needs you for success. You are always the main component of the hunting experience.

- You must be a *set-up artist*, setting your dog up for success through structured training which simulates the demands of actual hunting.

- Never give a command you are in no position to enforce. If you do, you're telling your dog it's okay to ignore your orders.

- Through hard work, you can have it all--the point, the handling, the retrieve, etc. You can have a finished gun dog if you want one.

- If you and your dog really don't like each other, you have a serious problem.

- All dogs, like human beings, can be better.

- You can always learn from others. Be receptive to new ideas and techniques.

- Read your dog's body language. He's reading yours!

- A good dog is a good dog. Breed, color, gender, and markings are irrelevant.

Chapter 13

- Be consistent, insistent, and persistent when training.
- Analyze the training process, teaching one command at a time.
- A little bit of praise at the right time will give your dog the feedback he needs for continued progress.
- Control your dog; don't let him control you.
- Expect good performance. Don't be satisfied with sloppy execution of a task.
- The retrieve is not an option--it is a requirement.
- Education is an on-going process. Learning continues throughout life--yours and your dog's.
- Start with a pup, not an older dog. There's no short cut.
- Your dog is not a machine. You must work with him yourself, even if you've had him trained for you.
- Your dog always knows when you're not paying attention to him. He'll take advantage of it too.
- You can't train your own bird dog without using actual birds in the training process.
- Most faults caused in a dog are man-made. For instance, dogs are not born gun-shy. They're made that way.
- Don't cop out by blaming your dog, his ancestry, the previous owner, or breed for problems unless you've first analyzed yourself, your techniques, your attitude, and your expectations.

14

The Right Tools
For Effective Training

You need to have the basic tools in order to do a job well. In the case of bird dog training, the following tools are necessary and should be procured before you start training:

Collar

- This should be of substantial construction, simple, $^3/_4$ to one inch in width. Nylon and leather are best. It is advisable to have your identification plate securely riveted to the collar. A choke chain collar is <u>not</u> recommended.

Photo 22 by: Terry Krueger.

The tools of the trade -- There's no substitute for using the right equipment. While you probably won't need all the equipment pictured on this table, you must use a checkcord and appropriate collar if you're to control your dog.

Photo 23 by: Terry Krueger.

The spiked force collar is essential to controlling a dog and to correcting learned faults. The discomfort caused by the studs is relieved once the dog complies.

Lead

- Your lead should be about six feet in length. Nylon and leather are best. A handmade braided poly rope lead works well. It should be of heavy construction so it won't kink up when being dragged.

Checkcord

- A 30 to 50 foot braided poly rope cord works nicely because it doesn't wrap around stubble or brush as easily as nylon rope.

Long lead

- This lead should be about 12 feet long. It is used on the dog after he's been trained on the long checkcord. The dog can be worked dragging this cord. He'll think you're still holding the other end. Use stiff braided poly rope. This can be handmade.

Whistle/lanyard

- Plastic is preferable to metal because the sound is more commanding. Besides, it is easier on your teeth and won't freeze to your lips during cold weather. The Acme™ is recommended.

Retrieving dummy

- This can be either canvas or hard plastic. A corn cob works well also for beginning retrieve training. Later on, you can wrap bird wings around either the dummy or corncob to combine *Fetch* with *dead bird training.*

Photo 24 by: Terry Krueger.

If you don't have the benefit of an assistant, the <u>whoa stake</u> is helpful in teaching a dog to remain in one location when told to <u>Whoa</u>.

Photo 25 by: Terry Krueger.

The use of the pigeon release harness with string makes it possible to control the bird in early gun dog training.

Blank training pistol

- The blank gun is used to get your dog accustomed to gunfire. As the bird flies, shoot the blank pistol so the puppy associates gunfire with birds.

Spiked force collar

- The Scott collar is recommended. It is a heavily constructed, thick nylon device with fairly dull studs. It can be ordered from several bird dog supply outlets as well as from the manufacturer.

Pigeon restraint harnesses

- Pigeons are great for training. The harness allows you to have complete control of the bird.

Quail and/or pheasant launch release traps

- By using these devices, you can simulate the actual hunting situation. The birds can be thrown up when you want them to fly.

20 gauge shotgun

- The lighter gauge gun is preferred when introducing dogs to gunfire.

Birds

- Pigeons are used to start training. However, you can also use them throughout the entire process if you wish. Instead of launching quail in the release traps, use pigeons.

Photo 26 by: Terry Krueger.

By using the mechnical (or electronic) bird launcher,
the trainer can control the timing of the bird's ascent.
By controlling both the dog (with the collar) and the
bird (with the launcher), it's possible to simulate a real
field experience while controlling all variables.

Photo 27 by: Terry Krueger.

By simply tripping the release lever, the bird is thrust into the air, ensuring flight.

Fishing rod with line and bird wing attached

- This is useful only in the early stages of training (sight pointing to teach *Whoa*).

Whoa stake

- If you don't have one of these devices, they are easy to make. If you don't wish to purchase or make one, you can teach *Whoa* by using either a small tree or an assistant.

Small wire cage

- This is used for carrying birds.

Frozen quail

- These can be used for working on the retrieve. Say "**Dead**" when throwing a frozen bird out for the dog to retrieve.

Ground cable

- 100 foot cable is preferred. This is a great device for training if you lack sufficient grounds to train or must train along a busy road. You can set birds along the side for the dog to point. It has many possible applications.

Electronic training collar

- This is optional and usually not needed. However, it will help you save time in case your dog has a seriously ingrained problem which needs correction. In lieu of purchasing this device, you might do well to find a professional trainer who could work with you for a fee, using his collar to correct your dog's serious problem.

Training table

- This is a useful device, traditionally used for training the Continental breeds. It is very effective for training all gun dogs to **Whoa**. It teaches patience and helps dogs accept training because they are somewhat less secure and must concentrate more while in this mental and physical state.

Using the right equipment in training will help prevent serious problems. The proper use of the equipment will ensure that your dog learns the correct way to handle birds in the field while working for you. If you lack the tools, you are inviting problems. If you have a bird dog, he should be trained. If he is trained, he should be trained right. When

Photo 28 by: Terry Krueger.
Wayne Colonnello's viszla, Gecka, is steady on point inside the flight pen. The spiked force collar and checkcord ensure that she learns that it's never permissible to charge into the bird.

your dog is trained right using the proper tools, you won't have to spend your time *re-training* him later. The right tools will help ensure that your dog learns things the right way and practices that way as well.

> *You can always learn from others.*
> *Be receptive to new ideas and*
> *techniques.*

15

Training

It's always easier to train than to retrain. If you want to develop a quality gun dog, analyze the training process and start from the beginning and progress toward the finished product one step at a time. Sounds easy, right? Well, it is, provided you really start from the beginning and build a firm foundation of behaviors which are reviewed, reinforced, and rewarded. The time to begin is when you first get your dog and teach him his name and make him aware of your acceptance of him as an individual, thereby imprinting on his mind the notion that his purpose in life is to nurture and preserve this acceptance. After he knows his name and realizes that he belongs to you, begin the yard training in which you focus on teaching your dog to *heel, whoa,* and *come* when called. All the while you're doing this, however, you're building a relationship with your dog which is based on love, acceptance, and fulfilled expectations. Each step of the training process is satisfying to you and your pup because you both gain satisfaction with each task learned. Because all complex activities build from the basics, thorough yard training is crucial to long-term success.

Heel

The best way to teach your dog to *heel* is to let him learn that the collar and lead will not hurt him. If he is a pup, let him wear the collar and simply drag the lead around for a while. Once you're satisfied that the lead doesn't distress him, you can hold the end and walk your dog around, making sure that he enjoys the experience. When you start training your dog to *heel*, use a conventional leather or nylon collar. Then switch to the spiked force collar provided your dog is big and strong enough to handle this device, a wonderful means by which you can keep your dog from lunging ahead, balking, and reacting to distractions around him.

It is customary to *heel* the dog on your left if you're right handed and on the right if you're left handed. To get your dog moving forward, give a slight tug on the lead. This causes the tightening spiked force collar to exert pressure to his neck. You want to make sure that the collar stops causing discomfort once the dog complies. For this reason it's important that the collar be properly put on the dog. The collar should slide through the end ring in such a way that the collar will loosen up once pressure is relieved.

When you start heeling, give the command *"Heel"* to get the dog moving forward. Proceed several steps this way. When you plan to stop, command *"Whoa"*, thereby reinforcing (through repetition) your command that the dog stop on *Whoa* and then resume walking when commanded *Heel*. Do this over and over again, praising frequently when the dog properly responds to the commands *Heel* and *Whoa*. If the dog

Photo 29 by: Terry Krueger.
Smokey was trained using the spiked force collar. Note that when the pressure is relieved, the collar loosens up.

doesn't want to stop on **Whoa**, apply pressure by tightening the spiked force collar. If he doesn't want to get moving on *Heel*, give a slight tug on the lead. Just be sure to check the collar, making certain that it loosens up each time the dog complies. Do not jerk harshly on the collar because your dog will soon respond when given slight tugs caused by your wrist action. You don't need to pull and jerk hard with your whole arm or body unless yours is a grossly undisciplined older dog who was never taught to *heel*. Always apply just enough force--not too much. Try to keep your lessons enjoyable for both the dog and yourself. During this stage it is important that the dog learn that he must always comply with your orders and reap the satisfaction of your praise when he *heels* and *whoas* nicely for you. To obey routinely is vital because future training sessions will be more complex. Let your dog get into the habit of abiding by your orders. There is tremendous carry-over value in all subsequent lessons.

If yours is a flush dog (retriever or spaniel other than a Brittany) you can have the dog *sit* when you stop. If you wish to teach the command *Hup* to a spaniel, you can give this command in place of *Whoa* or you can command *Sit*. In no case, however, should you encourage a pointing dog to *sit* at this stage. Teaching *Whoa* instead will facilitate teaching the next lesson.

Whoa

Every good pointing dog must *Whoa* on command. This is initially taught in conjunction with *Heel*, but it also has applicability for teaching a dog to hold point, back another dog, or simply halt when told to do so. Once *whoa* has been taught while heeling, the handler should be able to take a few steps away from the dog and command him to "*Whoa!*" In order to do this you must establish eye contact with your dog and maintain a serious, no-nonsense, facial expression while holding out the flat of your hand in a commanding, authoritative manner. If the dog remains stationary on *Whoa*, return to him and praise him,

Photo 30 by: Preston Crabtree.
Every good gun dog must <u>Whoa</u> on command. This is initially taught to puppies as they sight point. Mike Jenkins is giving three youngsters some practice. While the pups can charge into the wing, they find pointing more enjoyable. This is being reinforced by the soothing word W-h-o-a.

resuming *Heel* and *Whoa* together as a way of relieving pressure by returning to familiar learning. If the dog will not stay in place, catch him and briskly put him back in the original location. If this does not work satisfactorily, use the whoa stake, a device which you can push into the ground and thread a checkcord through. Take the dog to the vicinity of the whoa

Photo 31 by: Preston Crabtree.
Darcy, a Michigan-bred grouse dog owned by Preston Crabtree of Crabtree Kennels, Nashville, Indiana, pointing a grouse in Brown County, Indiana.

stake and pull the cord through, commanding the dog to "*Whoa*" after you walk away. Once again, be authoritative and establish a serious tone and eye contact. Once your dog knows that *Whoa* means *Halt* or *stay where you are*, you're ready to teach *Come* or *Come Here*.

Come Or Come Here

This command means come here <u>*now!*</u> If you see your puppy running toward you in order to get attention, take advantage of the situation and tell him to "*Come*," doing so with enthusiasm. While doing this, introduce the first whistle command, a single loud continuous blast on your whistle. While he's coming to you by his own choice at this point, your pup will learn that he is to come to you when told *Come* and/or when he hears the whistle. As you proceed with training, call your pup by saying "*Come*" or "*Come Here*" followed by your whistle signal. Encourage him to come in. If he doesn't come, quit telling him to do so. You don't want your dog to think he can ignore you. It's now time for a different method. Attach a checkcord to his collar. You could then use your whoa stake again, reviewing *Whoa*. Drop the cord and entice the pup to come in by calling "*Come*," followed by the whistle signal.

If you're lucky enough to have an assistant, ask that person to hold one hand on the dog's chest and one on his rump. The assistant must not talk to the dog or in any way distract him. You should then come up to the dog, look him right in the eye, command "*Whoa*" and walk away to the end of your 50 foot checkcord. Then command the dog to "*Come*," followed by the whistle command. As you do this the assistant is to push the dog off toward you as you simultaneously pull him in by the checkcord. Keep blowing your whistle the entire time, creating one long, continuous, obnoxious, steady blast until the dog comes in. Then reward and praise him lavishly. Repeat this procedure a few more times. In the future, you can use the whoa stake if your assistant is unavailable.

At this point your dog will *heel, whoa,* and *come* by following both a voice and whistle command. It's now time to advance beyond basic yard training. But while we're at this stage, let's introduce bird contact, starting first with a bird wing on the end of the fishing line. Flip the wing (*bird*) onto the ground, teasing and enticing the pup with it. Keep moving the *bird* around, saying "*Bird, Bird, Bird*" so the dog learns the meaning of *Bird*. Never let the dog catch the *bird*. However, when the dog points, leave the wing still, allowing the dog to savor the hypnotic ecstasy while on point. As you do this, reinforce *Whoa*, styling the dog up by stroking his tail or adjusting his stance. You can then, after a few minutes, flip

Photo 32 by: Len Jenkins.
Mike, a young pup by Charlen's Smokey, instinctively retrieves a pheasant to his owner, John Toman of Dearborn, Michigan. Mike was taught to come on command; retrieving is the next logical step. Note the slack checkcord.

the wing up and around saying "*Bird*" and making lots of noise as you do this. Be sure to keep the puppy excited. Drop the wing back to the ground and soothingly, yet commandingly, say "*Whoa.*" Style the dog up. Repeat the process a few more times. Just be sure to keep the pup happy. At this stage in the training you may want to introduce a pigeon just for the sake of building interest and excitement. Say "*Whoa!*" Style the pup. Let the pigeon fly up by snapping the restraint harness to release the *bird*. Make lots of noise. Keep the dog excited. Review calling him in. End by making him *heel*. Release him just before quitting so he can romp around and enjoy his experience and then put him away to think about the great time he's had. Boy, if this is *work* he'll be eager for more! What a life! Let's go to the field next so that we can build on our well-established foundation. At this time you should probably stop using the wing on the fishing rod since we don't want to make the pup dependent on sight pointing.

Quartering

Many dogs quarter naturally but still need a little training to develop this ground covering pattern. The cue to turn and/or go forward to hunt is two toots on the whistle. These toots should be snappy and cheerful, sufficient in themselves to instill enthusiasm. Note that this signal is much different from the heavy authoritative long blast commanding the dog to *Come*. Should your dog initially want to come in upon hearing the new signal, send him out again, making sure that there is no confusion in his mind as to what these two very distinct signals mean. Get your dog fired up and urge him to go forward, tooting twice. When he gets out twenty to thirty feet to the side, give two toots again and tug on the checkcord, this time using your spiked force collar. As you proceed across a field of short grass (so your line doesn't get tangled), zigzag in a way that you signal and tug on the checkcord so that your dog learns he is to cover the field in windshield-wiper fashion. Your pattern should be two toots--tug, two toots--tug, two toots--tug so he learns to turn eventually on the two toots, thereby preventing the discomfort caused by the tug.

You should periodically give him a long, hard blast to come in, thereby demonstrating for him the difference between these two signals. If he gets excited and seems reluctant to come in, give him a pull and the spiked collar will remind him that he is to obey this previously learned command. Praise enthusiastically when your dog masters the new signal and automatically turns on two toots. In order to refresh his memory, *heel* him in for the conclusion of the lesson, routinely giving him a *Whoa*, heeling again, and then perhaps sending him out again on a cheerful two-toots, only to be called back on the long blast! Now this is really putting the pieces to the training puzzle together!

You'll have to work your dog on quartering a few times before you can trust him to consistently go forward and/or turn on the designated signal. When you feel secure that he understands and will comply, drop the checkcord. Keep giving the signals to either turn or come in. If the dog misses his cue, run and step on the cord and give the proper tug. Just be quick about it! From then on as you're training, let the dog drag the checkcord. He'll never even know you're not actually holding the other end. When you're really confident in your dog, replace the 30-50 foot cord with one which is ten feet long. Once again you'll *fool* your dog and now he'll work nicely with less drag. The next step is to remove the short lead--and even the spike collar. Now you have a dog that consistently heels, comes when called, quarters and goes forward on command, works a field in a zigzag pattern, and searches for something *birdy*, to point. Let's go on to the next stage. The excitement builds--for both dog and handler!

Excitement Over Birds

Throughout the training process you should remind your dog that the name of the game is birds, birds, and more birds! This is done through frequently using the word *Bird* when your dog is around birds, or sees or smells birds. Make the dog use all his senses. He should hear the word *bird*, see the *bird*, and best of all, smell the *bird*. Now this is what a bird dog was bred for!

A good way to get a bird dog fired-up over birds is to snag a pigeon in a fishing net and tease, saying "*Bird, Bird, Bird,*" and then "*Whoa!*" At this point the dog should immediately freeze on point. This process should be repeated a few times. After your dog has had his memory refreshed, another technique you can employ is to take the pup <u>into</u> a pen of game birds, or even chickens. In this way the dog will once again hear the word *Bird*, see the bird, and then smell the bird--all at once. After this you should try a more challenging technique. Use your pigeon release harness and place a pigeon in high grass, out of sight but upwind of the pup. Let the pup go on point when you know he should smell the bird. You will know this because you will always work the dog <u>into</u> the wind. After the dog is on point, several feet from the hidden pigeon, lift the bird by the string and gently swing it in such a way as to lull the already pointing dog into an even more hypnotic point. Then, flush the bird by snapping the harness. As the bird flies off, make a lot of noise, trying to simulate the commotion your dog would hear if guns were fired. Do this several times. Before too long you'll be able to fire a blank gun and then a .410 or 20 gauge near your dog. Soon it will be time to shoot a bird over him, thereby showing him that the point really does culminate in total, absolute, unadulterated satisfaction. All the pieces to our puzzle are beginning to fit! It's now time to concentrate on the finer aspects of pointing. This is getting to be fun!

Pointing

If you've proceeded systematically in your training, your dog has already had some experience pointing (provided he is a pointing dog). Now it's time to fine-tune the point.

Whenever you work on pointing, use the words *Bird* and *Whoa* frequently. The dog should know that the word *bird* or a combination of words using *bird* means that birds are close.

Through repetitive work, your dog will learn to expect birds if you say something like *"Find The Birds!"* In the process of training, the dog will begin to trust you because there are indeed birds present when you say *"Bird."* Besides that, he'll enjoy the experience of bird contact so much that he will want to stay near you because he's associating your presence with birds. This in turn will help you develop a close-working dog. Now you will need to make sure birds are present.

We talked about style earlier, but now we're going to stress it. You need to plant birds upwind of your dog. Use pigeons for this. You can place about five of them in front of your dog in five separate locations. You'll be able to tell where they are because the blaze orange strings of the bird restraint harness will be visible to you, but not to the dog since he is color blind. When you notice the dog getting *birdy* as he approaches the first of your birds, command him to *"Whoa,"* applying a little pressure on the spiked force collar by pulling on the check-cord. Style up the dog. Improve his stance by making sure he's not leaning too far forward. Make sure his head and tail are up nice and high. Praise and sooth him so he knows that this is what you want. If his tail needs greater elevation, tap it lightly with the edge of your fingernail. If that

Photo 33 by: Charlene Jenkins.
The very beautiful Charlen's Magic Train pointing quail in Monroe, Michigan.

doesn't work, use a short saw blade, tapping the underside of the tail with the serrated edge. You can then keep your dog on point by walking in front of him and extending the flat of your hand, once again commanding *"Whoa."* If your dog wants to move, you can either use your whoa stake or ask an assistant to help you. Tease your dog by moving the bird, suspending it by the string. When you have done this long enough, snap the release harness, releasing the bird to fly away. If the bird's been trained to return to your pigeon loft, he'll be yours to use again. As the bird flies away, clap your hands, make a lot of noise, or fire a blank gun, in order to get your pup accustomed to noise. Now it's on to the next bird. Repeat the process until you have used up all five of your birds. You will notice that your pup's intensity and animation will improve. You'll also notice an improvement in his style on point since this is the object of your concern. As you work your dog in this manner, it's important that you keep improving because you'll want to maximize the return on all your set-up time. You'll notice that your pup will really like this.

Put your dog up for a while now and set out another five harnessed pigeons in a different location. In every case, make sure that the pigeon is hidden from the dog's view by grass or other vegetation. Besides working on style, you must also make sure that the dog is using his nose, not his eyes. Once again, work the dog upwind. Make him wind, seek out, and point each bird, making sure the points are firm and stylish and that he proceeds in a crisp, snappy manner as you work. Introduce a new element at this juncture in your training-- that is the call back (one long deliberate whistle blast) after allowing the excited dog to chase the released, flying bird a short distance. This is important because you'll establish in the dog's mind that he is to come back in after each bird find for you to acknowledge his achievement. If you don't establish this habit early on, you may end up with a dog that wants to pursue bird after bird, regardless of your desire. Such a dog would be in the next county by the time you catch up with him. Throughout practice your pup must:

- Seek out birds,
- Point with style (about 20 feet from the bird),
- Remain on point as you tease,
- Remain on point (steady to wing) as the bird flies or pursue the bird, depending upon your preference,
- Come back immediately upon your whistle blast, and
- Go back out to find more birds when given the two blast signal.

Do you see how all the pieces are starting to fit? It's all part of the overall picture and you'll be amazed at the dog's ability to assimilate each step and master the ever-increasing complexity of the complete process. Remember to make the dog do every little step exactly right. Be alert and vigilant so you don't inadvertantly leave out vital signals or cues.

In case you're still not satisfied with your dog's style, there are a couple of things you can do. If you have a training table, walk the dog up the ramp and allow him to point a plainly visible bird placed on the table. While the dog is on the table he's a little insecure and closer to your level. It's amazing how you can improve his points like this. Use the serrated saw blade and expect a perfect point. The dog should be standing proudly with legs securely under him with high head and tail and obvious interest, animation and intensity. Another technique that works nicely is teasing your dog with a pigeon in a net--such as one would use in landing salmon. Tease the dog saying "**Bird, Bird, Bird** "and let him pursue the bird visually and physically (you'll need an assistant for this). Periodically command "*Whoa.*" Style up the points, using the saw blade. Do this several times. It won't be long before your dog will do everything exactly right and do it in high style. Remember that *repetition and reinforcement* are *the name of the game.* You can have a close dog that points, holds, and handles to a tee. He'll also do all these things in high style.

Style is important. Try this lesson again until you *have it all.* Why not have the best? Right?

While this lesson is broken up in order to explain each of the elements, you should have developed your own sense of the training process by now because you understand your specific dog and the rudiments of training. Put it all together, utilizing your knowledge and common sense. Each dog, like each human being, is an individual. Work with your dog, building on each step, adapting as necessary, and always simulating what you really want in the field.

Introduction To Gunfire

Gun-shy dogs are not born; they are made. Shooting birds is the reward you'll reap from good dog work. It will do you no good if your dog handles easily, works the fields thoroughly and points stylishly, but runs for a place to hide when the gun is fired. Gun-shyness can ruin a dog and complicate all training. Therefore, prevent this problem by properly introducing your dog to gunfire.

Let your young pup get used to lots of noise. When he's on point or pursuing game birds, make noise as the bird goes up. If you're training a young pointer or setter to **Whoa** on point when working with the wing on the fishing rod line, make noise as you flip the wing into the air. You should also fire your blank pistol so your pup gets accustomed to the gun report when the *bird* flies up.

Once your pup is used to noise and does not react adversely in any way, you're ready to introduce him to the actual shotgun blast. To do this, you're first going to show him that the loud blast is nothing to fear. In fact, by the time we're finished, your young pup will associate the gun report with birds, expecting to find a downed bird whenever he hears gunfire. To get your dog to this point, you'll need an assistant. The entire process of getting the pup accustomed to and excited over gunfire takes only one well-staged training session. The tools for accomplishing this extremely important aspect of your dog's training are basic: a shotgun (.410 or 20 gauge preferred), at least one box of inexpensive shells, three birds (quail or pigeons), checkcord, and a spring bird launcher or release harness.

Here we go! We're going to prevent one of the worst problems of all through careful, systematic introduction to gunfire. Have your assistant, who obviously should be knowledgeable regarding firearm safety, go out into a field about two hundred yards and wait there for your signal--a nod of the head or the loudly yelled word "*Shoot!* " While you're with your dog in the original location, you should do everything possible to keep him in a relaxed, happy mood by playing with him and letting him do things he already knows well (*whoa, heel, come,* etc.). Your manner and voice must be very up-beat. While you're doing this, be noisy--clap your hands, talk loudly, blow the whistle or have another person talk loudly with you. Then signal to your assistant to fire into the ground, making sure that the blast is just one of many noises being made simultaneously. This way the dog hears gunfire while he's active and happy and comes to realize that this particular sound, like all the others he is hearing, is in no way frightening. Then walk toward the gun, making a lot of *happy* noise. As you do this, signal the shooter to fire, getting progressively closer until most of the rounds have been fired off. Keep up the happy noise. When you're about twenty feet from the shooter, signal him to fire. Come up to within five feet of the gun and signal again, having your assistant shoot another round or two. Keep up the *happy* noise by cheerful *fun talk*. If you do all this properly and if your dog has never had any adverse experience with gunfire, you're almost done with this lesson.

The next thing we need to do is to couple gunfire with birds. To do this you need to set out one of the birds in either the release harness or spring launcher. Work the dog in this direction, having your assistant hang back a short distance while you advance toward the bird by making lots of excited noise like "*Birds In Here*," or "*Find The Birds*," clapping as you go. Then have your assistant fire off another round. There should have been no negative reaction. As your pup approaches the bird, *Whoa* him into a point. (If he's a flush dog, keep up the noise and excitement by urging him on.) Flush the bird at the right time. Have the assistant shoot the bird, dropping it in front of the excited pup while you keep up the loud *fun talk* in an enthusiastic manner, yelling "*Dead! Dead!* "excitedly as the bird drops, running toward the dropped bird to excite the pup over this new experience. If all works out well, as it should, this will probably be an experience your dog will never forget, leaving in his memory an indelible imprint in which you and he were having a great time in the field. He located and handled a bird, the bird flew up and that wonderful, exciting sound (gunfire) was heard. Then the bird dropped to the ground, at which time you and your dog got very excited, and you praised him for a job well done! Wow!

Photo 34 by: Brad Belanger.
Thoropabst Lew poses with his prize. Lew was properly introduced to the gun by owner Brad Belanger of Royal Oak, Michigan. Lew performes to perfection!

This is getting better and better all the time! Set out the other two birds and repeat this procedure.

Now that your dog is accustomed to gunfire and realizes that the sound is heard in conjunction with falling birds, we're ready for the next step which has already been introduced (*Fetch*). We'll find the bird on the command **Dead**, thereby adding one more piece to our mosaic. Before long the picture will be complete, and you'll have a gun dog that will thrill you by his performance and dazzle you with his style. All this will be possible because you were careful and thoughtful in the way you introduced him to gunfire.

Using Birds In Training

We won't be able to effectively train your bird dog unless we provide him with plenty of bird contact. If we rely on wild birds alone, we're not providing enough predictable contact since we have no control over the birds' location or numbers. To further complicate matters, we have no control over the bird itself and have no guarantee the bird will even fly. In fact, oftentimes wild birds will run or just hide while other times they'll flush wildly and unexpectedly at the most inopportune times. Since we can't rely on wild birds, we'll have to provide your dog with bird contact by using pen-reared birds which we can control. After your dog has handled the tasks we've taught him through set-up bird contact situations, we can graduate him to wild bird work provided it is legal to run him on wild birds since most states prohibit this activity during the nesting season. Face it. There's no way to train a bird dog unless we use birds and eventually shoot birds over the dog. While providing birds for this purpose does entail some limited expense and trouble, the problems are not insurmountable. You can train exclusively with pigeons or start with pigeons and progress to quail, pheasants, coturnix, or chukars. While you should have no problem using pigeons or coturnix, the other birds enjoy legal status as game birds so you'll have to comply with your state's regulations regarding purchase, maintenance, possession, and use of game birds in order to keep your dog training activities on the right side of the law.

Pigeons

Pigeons are excellent for bird dog training. They are quite inexpensive and easy to keep. You can trap your own in barns or on city buildings by using traps or dead-falls. Commercially built pigeon traps are available from various manufacturers and distributors. If you don't want to trap your own pigeons or pay someone to do it for you, you can buy them inexpensively at livestock auctions or from pigeon breeders who want to get rid of their culls. While the maintenance of pigeons is discussed later in this book, you can just buy what you need and not bother with keeping your own flock. Many fine bird dogs have had all their early training exclusively on pigeons which were used in pigeon harnesses or spring-style bird launchers. The birds fly well, particularly if they were trapped from the wild, and make plenty of wing-flapping noise when launched, creating excitement for the dog. Pigeons are a good size for training. After you shoot one, you can freeze it and take it out periodically to work on retrieving with your dog. Pigeons are great for training--they're plentiful, legal, inexpensive, and cooperative. Take advantage of their easy availability and game bird qualities, and you can develop a classy gun dog, compliments of the common pigeon.

Coturnix

Photo 35 by: Tim Bryson.
Pigeons are excellent for training gun dogs. They're easily available, inexpensive, and cooperative.

The coturnix, also known as the Japanese quail, is suitable for bird dog training provided they are good, mature flyers. These birds are fairly inexpensive because they are easy to raise and lay eggs prolifically. If you use coturnix, be sure they're mature flyers since young under-developed birds are reluctant to fly, causing your bird dog training effort to fizzle.

Coturnix work nicely in the spring launchers. After your dog has worked them in launchers, you can set them out dizzied and provide practice and shooting over your dog as he hunts these birds. Since coturnix are generally not considered game birds in most states, you can shoot them over your dog anytime, provided of course you've checked your state's specific regulations in this regard.

Coturnix quail are very suitable for training; they're inexpensive and legal. They are also the right size, and they're easy to maintain until you're ready to shoot them. Give serious consideration to their use, and you'll be pleased with the results. Your dog will gain much experience at minimal expense to you.

Quail

Bobwhite quail are excellent for training your gun dog. While you have to follow your state's regulations relative to purchase, maintenance, possession, and shooting of pen-reared quail, these birds provide plenty of opportunity.

While it's best to begin training with pigeons in the pigeon release harness, you can graduate to quail sprung out of the launcher. Just position the bird in such a way that it will fly away from you. Have the dog work up to the bird. Then spring the launcher by stepping on the lever if yours is a pointing dog or pulling on a string if he's a flushing dog. A mature, flight-pen conditioned quail will fly strongly. As it does, make your shot, dropping the bird, and sending the dog out for the retrieve.

Quail are the perfect size for teaching early retrieving. Dog's really like them and you can feast of the shot birds at the conclusion of your training sessions. These birds are easy to maintain for short periods of time and are available from licensed game bird farms. Use a few quail in launchers at the conclusion of your training program and your dog's early bird-finding education will be complete.

Pheasants

This is an excellent bird for use in training except that they're expensive. Unless sprung from launchers, they sometimes refuse to fly and even when sprung they will sometimes just go up a couple feet and come back down to sit or skulk away. If you buy pheasant for immediate use in your training, be sure they're fully mature and flight-pen conditioned.

Because of the expense, you may want to use pheasants only in the final stages of your training. If you plan to hunt pheasants with your dog, give him

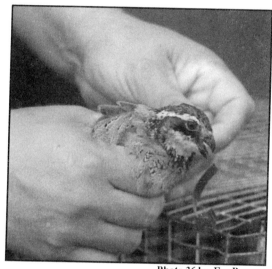

Photo 36 by: Eve Bryson.
Quail are useful in gun dog training. They are relatively inexpensive and "lost" birds may revert to the wild to help replenish wild populations.

exposure to this particular bird during training. You can start your training with pigeons and perhaps graduate to quail. Let your training program culminate with three or four raucous ringnecks sprung from a pheasant-sized spring launcher and your dog will benefit immensely. These birds are exciting to a dog and any prospective pheasant dog should have experience on pen-reared pheasants (even one) prior to being taken out in pursuit of the bird's wild brethren.

The problem with wild pheasants is that they don't play by the rules. They'll run, sit tight, skulk away or hide, but they often won't fly. Your dog will have to learn how to handle this crafty bird, but you can give him his first pheasant experience on a launched pen-reared bird that must cooperate. Launch such a bird, make the shot, and send the dog out to retrieve this big gaudy monster. After this experience you'll have a dog that wants more and more pheasant action.

Photo 37 by: Terry Krueger.

You can't train a pheasant dog without using pheasants in the training! In spite of their expense, pheasants serve a useful purpose in the training process.

Chukars

Chukars are useful for training in that they fly powerfully for good distances so you can make some excellent shots, giving your dog a better opportunity to practice marking falls. The chukar is a perfect size, being a compromise between quail and pheasants. While they're more expensive than quail and usually a little less costly than pheasants, they're worth using in spite of the cost, particularly if you are a grouse hunter. Chukars can be sprung from launchers positioned in the woods or brush land. You can set them out in such a way that they'll provide great practice for your dog and be a pretty good simulation of a flushing grouse. Just be sure that in using chukars in this manner you mark the location of your launchers and set them out in consideration of wind direction. If the dog you are developing is to be a grouse dog, you'll want him to point the bird from a sufficient distance, no closer than 30 feet. The chukar will work well for you in this regard and will be worth the expense.

Since chukars are legal game birds in some states, be sure to check regulations. There's no point in having your training session cut short by a visit from the local sheriff or conservation officer!

Locating And Retrieving Dead Birds

Bird dog training requires patience and forethought combined with good doses of common sense and honest effort. After thinking the process through and building on each step along the way, results will become evident. That's where we are right now. Our equation of :

patience + forethought + common sense + honest effort = a finished gun dog

is almost complete. So far, your dog comes when called, heels, whoas, points or pursues game depending on whether he is a pointing or flushing breed, tolerates the sound of gunfire without fear, fetches with enthusiasm, demonstrates general good manners, and loves earning your praise. We're now ready to fine-tune these skills even further and expand them to include the dog's actively locating and retrieving downed birds. The last piece of our puzzle is almost in place, and you will be the hunter in the picture we presented to you when you began reading this book. Let's put the last piece in place now.

The best way to develop a good retrieve in your dog, regardless of his breed, is to keep the retrieving exciting and stimulating. Since nothing is more exciting to a bird dog than birds, let's give him some action and let him retrieve birds which we will shoot over him in a simulation of a real hunt. This will, of course, take some preparation so you may want to ask someone to be your assistant in order to save time and facilitate this training. You'll also need the right equipment and birds so get everything ready first and formulate your strategy. You'll need three mechanical bird launchers which you can spring by stepping on the release lever, some short pieces of brightly colored plastic to mark the locations of your set-out launchers, a shot gun (preferably a 20 gauge), birds (quail or pigeons), your spiked force collar (Scott), whistle, 30 foot checkcord, safe grounds in which to shoot as you work into the wind, and a small wire cage to hold the birds until you get them loaded into the mechanical launchers. Because we want this first experience at locating and retrieving dead birds to be a successful simulation of a real hunt, be certain to allow plenty of time and make sure that your assistant fully understands your strategy. It's also advisable that you begin this training when there are no constraints such as excessively hot weather, rain, distractions, or lack of wind. Remember your dog will learn what he does so let's make sure nothing prevents him from doing all this right. Ready to start? Here we go.

Pointing Breeds

Start by doing a little basic discipline with your dog and reviewing his other skills such as quartering, responding to the whistle, getting excited, and searching for birds as you say "*Get*

The Birds." While you are doing this, have your assistant go out into the field and set out the three launchers so that they will be upwind of the dog as you work back to them. Keep the launchers at least 100 feet apart and staggered. They should also be somewhat covered with grass so as not to be excessively visible to the dog. Make sure your assistant identifies the location by placing a brightly-colored tag near each launcher. After the birds are set, you can work your dog back to them, working in their direction, moving toward the identifying tag, saying "*Bird, Bird, etc.*" By this time, your dog believes you because in the past we've always produced birds for him when we said *Bird*. As he approaches the first launcher *Whoa* him and get him on a good stylish point and have your assistant hold or step on the checkcord. Then look your dog right in the eye, extend the flat of your hand, say "*Whoa* "again, go in and flush the bird by stepping on the lever. As the bird goes up, shoot it, letting it drop in front of the dog so he can see it fall and learn to mark a shot bird. Then enthusiastically say "*Dead, Dead, get the Dead Bird*," urging him forward. He'll mouth the bird. As he does this be quick because timing is of the essence here if you want a natural retrieve. As he gets the bird in his mouth, say "*Fetch*," pull in his cord gently as you blow the whistle to make him come in. Don't jerk him. Be firm and steady. When he brings in the bird, make a big fuss over him, telling him to *Give* as you take the bird from his mouth. Then for practice, throw the bird out and up a few feet, letting it drop in front of your pup. Say "*Dead*," urge him out, say "*Fetch*" as he picks up the bird, and call him in on *Come* and a long whistle blast. Praise him as you say "*Give*." Do this three or four more times so that your dog learns to mark the falling bird's location and to know the meaning of *Dead*, the only command on which it is permissible for him to put the bird into his mouth. Next go on to the second and third birds which you placed in the field and repeat the process. Your dog should be very enthusiastic having had so much exposure to birds which were actually shot over him, bringing the hunting experience to fruition. Assuming that all went well and that your dog was steady to wing and shot (thanks to your spiked force collar and previous effective training), you can start the whole cycle over again if you wish by setting out three more birds. First, however, take the dog out into the field to search for more birds, wild ones this time. Work on basic discipline again if the excitement has made him a little difficult to manage. Then rest your dog a bit, get him a drink, and indulge and talk to him so you can both savor the pleasure and satisfaction you've just experienced. After a brief rest you can start training again, knowing that you've got three more birds waiting for your dog to find, point, remain steady to wing and shot, mark where they fall, locate them once hit, and retrieve to hand. You now have a bird dog which has tasted the pleasures of the hunt. He'll keep getting better and better, provided we keep all further experience constructive and consistent through proper training and hunting simulations. After a little more work, your dog will be ready for wily Iowa pheasants, flighty Michigan grouse, or explosive Georgia quail. We'll be ready for the real thing!

Flushing/Retrieving Breeds

If you are using a flushing dog such as a springer or one of the retriever breeds, you'll have to adjust the training process since your dog must wind the bird and then proceed toward it to make the flush. Since you'll want the bird to flush just before your dog gets to the launcher, you'll have to tie a 20 foot string to the spring release lever so that you can bend down and pull the string before the dog gets to the launcher. You might want your assistant to do this as well as hold your dog's checkcord so you can concentrate on making the shot. It's crucial that the timing is right and that you shoot the bird so <u>concentrate</u> on what's happening. Take your time as necessary to assure that this simulation is consummated to perfection. Once the bird is shot, send the dog out on the command **Dead**. When he mouths the bird, command "*Fetch*," then "*Come*" and give one long whistle blast while gently pulling the checkcord to bring the dog in. Command "*Give*" and praise ecstatically for retrieving to hand. Throw the bird up and out again, commanding "*Dead, Come, Fetch, Give,*" and repeat this process a few more times. Then go on to the other birds you have set, repeating the process. With a little more practice, you and your dog will be ready for the crafty birds out in the wild. The simulation is like the real thing in slow motion. The real thing, though, is a lot of fast, furious action. If your dog does it right in training, he'll learn to handle wild birds. Teach him the basics in a controlled setting. Let the wild birds teach him the rest. He'll have to be smart and well-prepared to handle that!

Fetch

We should introduce your dog to the joy of retrieving early in his education. Very few dogs refuse to retrieve and all can be improved in this area. The trick is to make your pup enjoy doing it because it brings immediate gratification--your praise. To start your pup out, he should first know the command **Come**. Then you should throw out an unfamiliar light-weight object like a corn cob or small retrieving dummy. Throw the object to be retrieved only a few feet. It's best to have your pup on a short checkcord. We need to get him enthusiastic by using a happy voice and by making a game of this task. Throw it out, saying, "*Get it! Fetch*" etc. When he gets the object in his mouth, call him in. If he doesn't comply,

Photo 38 by: John Laney.
John Laney of Newport, Michigan directs his well-trained springer, Molly, into a northern Michigan grouse covert. Molly responds to whistle, hand, and voice signals.

go to him and take it out of his mouth, saying "*Give.*" Throw it out again. Your pup will soon learn that in order to perpetuate this game, he has to relinquish his object (corn cob, dummy, or ball) on command. Repeat this process numerous times. All the while this is done you must say, in an enthusiastic tone, "*Get it, Fetch, Come, Give, good dog!!! All right!*" Then do it all again. What fun!

Your dog will naturally want to put an interesting, light-weight object into his mouth, particularly when he associates this object with play-time. Make sure you use the same object each time so he makes the right associations. Never let him just have his *toy* at times when you're not teaching this command because we don't want your pup to become bored with what might become a common-place object. The object to be retrieved must remain special--something he looks forward to bringing in to you and for which he's given lavish praise and a good time. Keep the early retrieving light and fun. Before too long it will be time to put more pieces together and couple the command *Fetch* with other signals in the advanced training such as "*Whoa, good boy*," as you go in to flush and shoot real birds. When the bird comes down and as the dog marks its fall, you'll command "*Dead or Dead Bird.* " When he goes to mouth the fallen bird, you'll then command "*Fetch*," then as he brings it in, "*Give*." But in order to get to this point, you have to start from the beginning, making sure that your pup enjoys retrieving by rewarding him each time he does it right. To help ensure that everything goes right, you should:

- Remain enthusiastic.
- Let your pup drag a short lead.
- Gently, but firmly, pull him in by the lead if he's reluctant to come in when called.
- Call him in firmly yet cheerfully.
- Praise enthusiastically when he comes in when called (with the object in his mouth) even if you had to pull him in.
- Tell him to "*Give*," taking the object from his mouth.
- Praise again for compliance to "*Give*," even if you had to take the object from him.
- Let him see the object as you enthusiastically throw it out again, letting him mark the fall as you repeat the process.

   If your dog does not want to come in with the object when called, you can work him on a ground runner, preventing him from romping around with the object. After all, we want your dog to play this game by our rules, not his, just as we will expect him to play by our rules when actually hunting.

Backing

A pointing dog working the field and suddenly going on point in high style is an exciting sight to behold. A brace of fine dogs, however, working as a team is awesome, particularly when one goes on point and the brace mate stops dead in his tracks to honor the point.

You will want your dog to honor another dog's point because it shows nothing more than bad field manners if he won't. If you let your dog steal another dog's points, you won't be getting many more invitations to go hunting with fellow hunters who also own a good dog. They won't appreciate your dog's going in front of another dog's established point, stealing the point, and causing jealousy and rivalry at a time in which stealth and careful bird-handling are in order. The bird will most likely flush prematurely if two dogs are competing to see which will get there first, creating commotion as both get too close to the bird. This kind of situation will result in a missed opportunity. You wouldn't like it if another dog did this to your dog on point so make sure your dog doesn't do it either. You need to teach your dog to **back (honor)** another dog's point.

A backing dog is, in essence, a dog pointing another dog which is on point. In order to get your dog to do this, you're going to need another dog which handles well and will remain on point in spite of the distraction you might cause making your dog go on point behind him. If you don't have access to a finished dog that will permit this, you can use another inexperienced (*green*) dog like yours or a plywood cut-out silhouette of a dog on point. While working on backing, it is essential that your dog already knows how to **Whoa** on command and that he does not get wild around birds. For this reason, backing shouldn't start until the dog has had some experience. Since even a well-started dog may get jealous and want to crowd the bird by going in front of the dog on point, you must use your spiked force collar and a checkcord which the dog can drag. Should he get too close to the pointing dog, you'll at least be able to reach down for the cord and give it a tug or apply light pressure as you command the dog to "*Whoa*," well back of the first dog. By using the spiked force collar you'll be able to stop your dog easily and still have good control of him without talking to excess, thereby possibly unnerving the first dog.

In order to teach your dog to back, you are going to have to do some extra preparation beyond simply having another dog present. The first requirement is to begin this training on restrained (caged or harnessed) birds because it's difficult to rely on wild birds since you have no control over when or how they fly. In fact, sometimes a wild bird won't fly at all but rather run away. The second most important aspect of this kind of training is a good wind into which you can work the dogs. Having the right equipment (cages, spring launchers, harnesses, etc.) is crucial. Keep in mind that in getting started with this kind of training you have to plant the birds upwind. Then bring the dogs, yours and preferably one more experienced than yours, up toward the bird. After the experienced (*front*) dog goes on point, you'll have to bring yours to a point and sooth him to remain so. Then you have to either flush the bird or in some way let the dogs know that this experience has really culminated in a bird-find so they can get some pleasure and satisfaction from it. Next, you have to call the dogs in for acknowledgement and praise and send them out again to repeat the process. There's much involved. Since you only have one pair of hands, you will need at least one or two assistants to make this type of training possible. There's a lot to manage, and there's a good possibility that something

Photo 39 by: Len Jenkins.
Steve Thompson, a professional shooting preserve guide from Bowling Green, Ohio, assists at one of the writer's training clinics. Rambo, owned and trained by Christine Tabone, is on point with John Podczerwinsky's brilliant German shorthaired pointer, Tasha, backing.

could go wrong. Don't risk having your dog's first experience with backing fail. Remember that the dog will learn what he does--right or wrong. Be prepared to make him back correctly.

Teaching a dog to back consistently is a complicated process because of the many possible constraints with which you must deal. Let's just say that you are ready to start and that all elements are satisfied. You have another dog, the pen-reared birds, the equipment (cage, launchers, harnesses, collars), the wind, and the necessary helpers. Let's say that you have already allotted sufficient time to this training so that you can give <u>both</u> dogs a satisfying experience and remedy any possible problems which might unexpectedly arise. If you're ready to start, here it goes, step by step:

- Place a couple of pigeons or quail in a small wire mesh cage, perhaps 2 feet by 3 feet in size. This cage must be placed upwind from the direction you will be working the dogs. Be sure to mark the location of this cage so you don't spoil your set-up by coming into it obliquely, running the risk of having the dogs point it too close. Remember, you do not want the dogs so close that they see the cage. This cage should be hidden in grass. You should mark the location by tying a small blaze orange piece of plastic to a nearby weed or bush. It would be wise for you to set out two or three cages, marking each clearly so you can systematically have the dogs find, point, and back. Having more than one set-up will assure that you can reinforce the learning which needs to take place. The multiple set-up also increases efficiency because less time is lost between pointing experiences since you won't be going back and forth planting the cages of birds.

- Next you get the dogs. It's important that your dogs handle easily as you do this so warm up by first working on a little discipline. Expect good compliance to the whistle commands and work on **Whoa** a bit by coupling this with **Heel.** Also **Whoa** the dogs by commanding "**Whoa.**" Then walk away. Call them in and talk to them as necessary. With all the set-up time involved in teaching backing, you won't want your dog to mess things up by temporarily forgetting the fundamentals. After the brief warm up, work the dogs in the field, but not in the immediate vicinity in which you placed the cages. Let the dogs get excited as they quest for birds. Be sure they are quartering satisfactorily and that they are responding to your whistle. This is no time or place for any wildness. Next swing the dogs around toward the first cage. Observe them carefully and get ready to act when they are making game. Be sure one dog (the more experienced) is in front. When he goes *on point*, immediately command the less experienced dog to **Whoa**, but make sure he sees the first dog on point. Sooth both dogs. Apply a little pressure by pulling lightly on the checkcords they are dragging, letting the spiked force collars remind them that they are to remain only in that precise location on a staunch point. Once both dogs are on point, have your assistants hold each to make sure neither breaks point. Then walk forward. Turn around. Remind them to remain on point by giving them another **Whoa**, also using the extended flattened hand and good eye contact to let them know you are serious. Then raise the cage excitedly, encouraging by yelling "*Bird! Bird!*" Drop the cage. Then allow the dogs to break point and go to the cage. Get excited as you release them from their points. The birds inside the cage will help by fluttering wildly. If you've planted one or two more cages, finish out this procedure by repeating it. The young dog should learn that he will get satisfaction whether he is the first or second dog. This set up should be done on only one training session because you don't want your dog to think that birds don't fly when you're expecting him to back. This procedure is for training purposes only. We are now ready to graduate to something which more nearly simulates real hunting.

- On a different day on which you have good wind, another dog, and a couple of friends to assist, you can continue your dog's backing education in a more realistic manner. Place a quail or pigeon in each of three mechanical or electronic spring launchers. Place the loaded spring launching devices out in the field as you did the cages previously. Be sure to mark their locations with a brightly colored piece of plastic. Let the launchers remain set out for a short while but make sure that they're not in the hot sun if you are training in the summer. These launchers should be in high grass (at least 12 inches) so as not to be easily visible to the dog. By this stage in the game we want scent pointing only. After your field has been set, go get the dogs and warm up again as you did when you set out cages. No wildness is tolerable so review all commands. Take the dogs into the field, telling them to "*Find The Birds*" with lots of enthusiasm in your voice. Swing them around to the part of the field where you've planted the launchers. Have the more experienced dog in front. When the less experienced dog sees him snap to a hard point, command "*Whoa!*" Have your assistants hold the check cords, applying a little pressure to remind the dogs that they are to remain on point in the exact locations they're in now. Once again step forward, establish stern eye contact, extend the flattened hand as you say "*Whoa.*" Go forward and launch the bird by tripping the spring if yours is a mechanical launcher or pushing the button if it's electronic. Make a lot of noise on the flush, perhaps clapping your hands, yelling "*Bird*," or shooting a blank pistol. Let the dogs get excited. If the dogs break, command them back with the long whistle blast. Praise lavishly. Then send them out again with two short toots to find the next bird. As you continue to the next cage, do this a few more times, letting the dogs alternate between being the front dog and the backing dog. Once they realize that the experience is satisfying, you won't have one dog creeping forward to steal a point. You'll also establish in the inexperienced dog's mind that he will be rewarded if he takes advantage of respecting another dog's point.

Photo 40 by: Frank Tabone.
Christine Tabone's Rambo backing a training model constructed by the owner. This model, painted in acrylics, is very realistic. A backing dog is in essence a dog pointing another dog. Such a dog must be taught to <u>Whoa</u> on command.

This should do it relative to backing but you'll have to reinforce and polish the process as you combine it with skills your dog still has to master. Try to keep the backing process in mind. After introducing gunfire, have your dog mark the fallen birds, search for cripples or dead birds when commanded *Dead*, retrieve when commanded *Fetch*, and **Give** to release the retrieved bird to hand. Repeat the backing lesson. This time we'll do it with a dog that's nearly finished. We're on the way to having a finished gun dog, one that *does it all*. We'll get to this point one step at a time, always building on previously mastered bird-handling skills. Piece by piece, you'll have a quality gun dog that will consistently and masterfully give his best.

Never give a command you are in no position to enforce. If you do, you're telling your dog it's okay to ignore your orders.

16

Correcting Faults

There is no place in dog training for discouragement because this negative feeling will also transfer to the dog in one way or another. Yet discouragement could affect us if something goes wrong in the training process in spite of our patience, forethought, common sense, and honest effort. Faults can crop up to our dismay so we'll either have to accept them or correct them. Since we've gone into our dog training venture optimistically, we need to reaffirm our commitment to our task by reflecting on two basic premises. The first is that all dogs, like people, can be improved through planning, commitment, and hard work. Faults can be corrected; if they are serious enough to interfere with the dog's performance, we had better find the remedy if we don't want to settle for second-best. The second premise is that dedicated sportspeople like us can *have it all.* If we want a gun dog that will handle, point, honor, obey, and retrieve to perfection and do it all in high style, that's what we'll have if we want it. Second-rate might be good enough for some, but not for us!

No single dog will suffer from all the flaws and faults described in this chapter. However, one or two of these might become evident in any dog in case something goes wrong somewhere in the training. While we've always practiced the best training techniques, perhaps you inadvertently communicated the wrong signal to your dog, and he did something wrong. Realizing that dogs learn what they do, whether right or wrong, and that each time something's done it is reinforced, we had better tackle the fault immediately. We'll tackle the problem assertively and thoughtfully while maintaining high expectations, bringing out the best in the dog and ourselves. Serious faults are unacceptable. We will accept and expect only the best.

Gun-shyness

This is a man-made flaw caused by an unfortunate experience. Most secure dogs accept noise easily, but insecure ones sometimes can't tolerate loud noise without becoming frightened. If your dog has been reprimanded in some way and learned to cower or cringe when hearing a loud noise, you might have a dog prone to gun-shyness by prior conditioning. By the same token, if your dog has been *babied* to excess and protected from noise by extreme measures to insulate him from all noise-induced stress, you might, likewise, have a gun-shyness candidate on your hands. If you've noticed your dog's softness and have carefully introduced gunfire so as to prevent gun-shyness as recommended earlier, you've been thoughtful indeed. But a soft dog, in spite of all your efforts, might still become gun-shy if you're not careful enough. If your dog is gun-shy, let's try something new, realizing that it's going to take a lot of time and positive handling. There is no room in our training strategy for anger or discouragement.

The first thing we need to do is let the dog know that noise in itself won't hurt him. Clap your hands, talk loudly, and generally let your dog associate background noise with the pleasures of going afield. Talk more loudly when you play with him also. Clap your hands, blow the whistle louder, drop things so they make noise, shut car doors loudly, etc. Do this over a long period of time. This way the dog will learn to accept noise because he realizes no harm comes to him by noise in itself. In fact, we've shown him that he can enjoy himself in spite of loud background noise.

Once your dog accepts loud noise, begin introducing gunfire, but start light. Clap your hands and make noise your dog's accustomed to hearing when he's working in a field or while occupied with something interesting a good distance away from you. When doing this, fire a blank gun combining the shot sound with the clapping. In this way you're teaching him to accept gunfire as just another sound which won't hurt him. Continue this procedure a few more days, getting progressively closer to your dog when combining the gun report with the clapping and other noise. Don't overdo it. A little medicine at a time can cure an illness while an overdose can kill. Let's not overdose your gun-shy dog and set back your progress. Easy does it. We've got plenty of time to bring a fine dog around.

After your dog accepts the blank gun report without flinching, go out into the field with him, making lots of noise and maintaining lots of excitement and happy talk. Ask an assistant to stay back and fire a gun, perhaps a .22 caliber rifle or .410 or 20 gauge shotgun when signaled to do so. Let your dog romp around excitedly but make sure he's not on birds (we don't want to inadvertently cause bird-shyness!). On your signal, at just the right time, have your assistant fire a round. Continue making noise and being excited with your dog. By ignoring the shot (which was still blended in with a lot of background noise) you're communicating to your dog that the gun report is nothing to fear. Remain in the field with your dog and have your helper fire another round, and then another, as he progressively gets closer and as you continue the background noise and happy talk. Once again don't over-do this. Enough is enough. Tomorrow is another day.

If your dog accepts this gunfire without fear, it's time to change course. Ask your assistant (one who also has good rapport with your dog) to fire a 20 gauge shotgun when signaled by you with a nod of the head. Have him begin this procedure about 150 yards away. While the dog is happy, both you and the assistant should make a lot of noise talking in a friendly, excited way and clapping. On signal, your assistant can fire a round into the ground, getting progressively closer. He should shoot again and again, blending the gunfire with all the happy, non-threatening background noise. If it appears that the dog can take this, keep it up. Hopefully your dog will continue to accept this. The last shot, perhaps the last round from the box, could be fired ten feet or so from the dog. Make sure this closest shot is not fired into the ground in such a way as to cause dirt to hit the dog in the face.

If you've been patient and brought your dog to accept gunfire without fear, it's now time to combine gunfire with birds. Because we don't want your dog to associate a frightful sound with birds, we've left birds out until now since bird--shyness, the next problem we'll address, is even more difficult to remedy than gun-shyness. So far in our re-education of the dog regarding gunfire, we've shown him that gun report is a non-threatening, harmless background noise, thereby letting him maintain a neutral attitude toward the sound. In combining gunfire with birds, however, we're going to make your dog realize that birds, something he likes, are always associated with the sound of guns.

We must be very careful now. Set out a pigeon in a bird release harness. Allow your dog to find it. Let him go on point if he's a pointing breed or flush the bird if your dog is a flushing breed. Release the pigeon. As it flies away, have your assistant, who is standing back some distance, fire a blank as you excitedly clap your hands, saying *"Bird,"* etc. Do this a few more times if your dog seems to be adjusting satisfactorily to the sound of gunfire coordinated with a bird going up. Continue this procedure a few more times, preferably on a different day. Then replace the blank gun with a .410 or 20 gauge. Repeat the same process. Before you know it, you'll be ready to shoot a bird, showing your excited dog that gunfire is essential to his full satisfaction and yours. Without the gunfire, the bird can't drop. Your dog will soon anticipate gunfire in a positive way and search actively for downed birds when the gun goes off.

Patience pays. If you want to cure gun-shyness, be patient and realize you're going to have to go slowly and thoughtfully. There's no other way. Easy does it!

Bird-shyness (blinking)

This is a very difficult problem to correct, but results are possible assuming that your bird dog has interest in birds bred into him. Since bird-shyness, like gun-shyness, is caused, it's best to prevent it than to deal with it once it's affected your dog. If you start out with a pup and train according to the principles and methods outlined in this book, you should not have a bird-shy dog except as a possible consequence of improper or hasty introduction to gunfire. But if you bought an older dog, it's possible that something happened to make him bird-shy. If your dog is bird-shy, try to figure out what unfortunate experience with birds caused him to fear them. Perhaps your dog was hit in the face with a bird wing he was pointing when he was a pup. Or possibly someone may have reprimanded him by whipping him with a dead bird. Perhaps he was slapped in the face by a spring launcher as a bird flew up because the trainer let the dog get too close to the launcher. If your dog was spurred in the face by a crippled pheasant he was trying to retrieve at too young an age, he might have suffered such trauma that he may never fully recover. Investigate. Experiment. Observe. Try to figure out what probably caused the problem and then work this into a strategy for correction.

If your dog will work a bird and then shy away when he gets close, you have some hope. Encourage your dog. Let him pursue or point the birds he's winded but don't let him get close to them. You can control this by setting birds out in electronic launchers. Stop your dog about 30 feet from the bird. *Whoa* him. Launch the bird and let him watch it fly, perhaps even charging it. Do this over and over as necessary. If he's not also gun-shy, you can fire a blank gun. Let your dog learn that birds won't hurt him. Instead, they're the quarry--a source of great fun. Eventually, let your dog get closer to the bird. If you're getting good points or active interest from a flush dog at about twenty feet from the bird, there's a pretty good chance you'll bring the dog around.

After your dog shows some interest in birds, shoot one over him (only if he's not gun-shy as well). Let him see that the shot bird can't hurt him and that handling the bird as he's done has brought you great satisfaction which results in lavish praise for him. Be sure to use only pigeons in curing a bird-shy dog. These small, gentle birds won't intimidate a bird-shy dog as much as pheasants would.

While you can actively work on bird-shyness, you can also address the problem passively. If your dog is terrified by birds and tries to avoid them, make him live near birds so he learns that they can't hurt him. Tie such a dog out next to a bird pen. If you can't maintain a pen of pheasants, quail, or pigeons, perhaps you can get some chickens and set them out in a pen just a few feet from your dog. Feed and water the dog in such a way that he must approach the chickens, coming close to them to get his food and water. He should soon learn that they can't hurt him. In fact, he may even take a special interest in them as he watches their movements. If this is the case, tie him on a ground runner and let him cavort freely down the line. It will make him progressively bolder around the chickens.

If you don't want to construct a pen by your dog, you can cover his kennel with nylon mesh and make a little perch a few feet off the ground. Then put a couple of domestic pigeons in his pen. The pigeons will come close to the dog, and he will learn to accept and ignore their presence although eventually he will take an interest in them, particularly if you let him get bored. The main problem with putting pigeons in the pen with your dog is that they will soil his food and water. To prevent this, don't feed and water your dog free choice. Instead, set out his food and water on a schedule. If he's hungry and thirsty enough, he'll eat and drink in spite of his anxiety over the pigeons. If you find that he starts getting aggressive with the pigeons as they come toward his food and water, you've witnessed a good sign. If he gets mad enough to chase the birds off or even attacks and kills the marauders for laying claim to his food and water, you might have a bird dog who some day pursues birds, instead of fleeing from them.

If your bird-shy dog has the problem to the extreme and refuses to demonstrate any interest in hunting, perhaps he's not bird-shy. Perhaps he is just not interested in birds and hunting. If this is the case, try your best to encourage him. But if he's not a bird dog at heart, regardless of his breed, he's just not a bird dog; and you would be better off starting with a new prospect. If your dog is animated and athletic and formerly showed interest in birds and currently shows some interest as long as the birds aren't too close to him, there is hope that you can help your dog overcome the scourge of bird-shyness, the most difficult of all problems to correct.

Trailing

If your dog plays follow-the-leader and simply trails another dog while out in the field, you have a man-made, correctable problem. The unfortunate thing about this, however, is that it's a shame you have to spend time and energy correcting something like this. Many people believe that a young dog can be taught to hunt by merely taking him out with an older, more experienced dog. While this may help develop a young dog if it is done at the right time and under the right circumstances, more often than not it will cause a young dog to trail.

It's usually best to work only one dog at a time. If you wish to work two, make sure they're the same age and size and that one does not follow while one leads. Dogs, even trained brace mates, must hunt independently except for honoring each other's points. Don't inadvertently cause trailing by running two dogs together in the early stages of training.

If your dog trails, you can break him of this in a variety of ways. The best way is to take him out individually so he learns that he must search for birds actively if he wants any action.

Another good way is to take a trailing pup out with two or more other pups of similar size. The trailing pup will get confused and not know which pup he wants to follow. After several distractions and much indecision, he just might give up this silliness and begin working on his own.

If all else fails and your young dog insists on trailing, more drastic measures are needed. There are still a couple of possible cures. Try to locate a good, close-working hunting dog who will not tolerate trailing and other such nonsense in the field. Take the young pup and the experienced dog out together. If the young trailing pup approaches too closely, the older experienced dog will most likely growl or in some other way communicate that this foolishness (trailing) is to stop now. If the trailer insists on trailing, let the older dog get into a scuffle with him and put an end to this follow-the-leader foolishness once and for all. Just be sure, of course, to be close by so that the trailer doesn't get seriously hurt. In all probability, a few aggressive nips will cause the pride to suffer more than the body. The discomfort to the trailing dog is a small price to pay for the immense rewards to be gained from a classy, bold gun dog that hunts independently of his brace mates. If you can't locate another dog to help cure your pup of trailing, there's always the electronic collar. Before using the electronic collar, however, please refer to the next chapter, *The Shock Collar*, regarding the proper use of this training device. Since your dog already understands the command *No!*, order him to stop by saying "*No!*" If he refuses to stop trailing, give him a light jolt as he trails. In order to curb him of sticking too closely to another dog, you may have to give him a little shock if he insists on continuing. He'll then associate the discomfort of the electric shock with the dog he is trailing. This in itself should cure the problem.

Whatever you do, don't accept trailing. If you own and feed two dogs and one of them is a trailer, you would be better off owning only one (the one who actually hunts). The trailer is nothing more than dead weight. You can get rid of the trailer, or you can get rid of the problem. If you really like the dog, in spite of his trailing, the problem is curable. Remember, you can *have it all*, even a brace of class gun dogs, each pulling its own weight. Why not?

Running Too Wide

This is an annoying problem because it causes anxiety for you, the owner/trainer/hunter. The problem is that you know you have an aggressive, assertive dog working as hard as he can to produce game for you. However, given today's hunting conditions, an out-of-range gun dog can cause you either to trespass on property or worry about your dog because he might be locked up on point at some distant location and require your protracted search in order to find him. A dog's running too wide is a real impediment to your fully enjoying the hunt. Besides the risk of trespass litigation and your anxiety over a lost gun dog of great value, you miss the pleasure of watching your dog work the coverts in search of your favorite game bird. Remember, once again, you can *have it all*. Let's bring that bird-finding dynamo of yours into range--ours!

The best way to prevent this problem is to restrict the dog completely in his early training and, once fit for hunting, throughout the hunt. Don't cut him any slack, ever! Keep him in range, always! Use the whistle. If he can't be trusted to hunt close, slap on the spiked force collar and let him drag a fifty-foot checkcord. Dogs learn what they do. If you let him get out too wide, he's learning to do it that way. Don't let him do it <u>ever</u> even if it means you can't relax and enjoy the hunt. A dog running too wide is of no use to you unless perhaps you are on horseback, in a jeep, or have your dog equipped with a beeper collar, provided, of course, you have permission to hunt on all land within a significant radius of the location at which you begin your hunt.

An out-of-range, big running dog is typically an aggressive dog with an all-consuming desire for birds. Such a dog will reach out far to find birds and if he locks on point and holds for you, his manner is not at all objectionable in wide-open country. If you're in good physical condition and are not averse to working hard and fast on your hunts, such a dog might be just what you need. If on the other hand you hunt in thick, rough country and don't have legal access to vast expanses of territory, such a dog will not meet your particular needs.

Besides being wide, some big runners literally over-run the birds and cause excess numbers of birds to be lost to your gun because the dog has bumped them. To complicate matters further, some of the real wide running dogs will not obey when they're way out in the field. Even if they hear your whistle, they sometimes feign deafness, perhaps thinking that you're too far away to notice them and too incapable of reprimanding for misconduct. If you want to avoid a lot of headaches, insist that your dog work in close.

If you've done everything possible to develop a close-working dog yet find that he still ranges out too far, you may have to use the electronic collar. Please read the next chapter, *The Shock Collar*, on the use of the electronic collar before actually using it, however. In order to shorten up such a dog's range, you must reinforce the notion that there's always a penalty for disobeying your whistle (two toots). That penalty is the shock. Before starting this correction, review for the dog what he's supposed to do, using old-fashioned methods with your trusted spiked force collar. When the dog is distracted, put on the shock collar. Take him out and work him, tugging on the checkcord when you give the commands, causing the spiked force collar to inflict some discomfort. Keep working the dog. Then give him a command to turn before he gets out too far. This time give him a shock. Your dog might get scared though and either run off or run toward you. If it appears he might run off, make sure you catch the end of his checkcord. Before too long, your dog will consistently work closer, paying attention to your whistle. He'll soon learn that getting too far out and not minding the whistle results in a shock. The benefit to accrue from doing this in conjunction with the standard spiked force collar is that the dog may never know which collar actually renders the shock. Try to deceive him as long as possible in this regard since he may only comply when the collar is on if he ever becomes *collar wise*.

You should be able to shorten your dog's range. Some dogs will be harder than others, but all can be improved. If you find that your dog is both too wide and too fast for your preferred hunting style yet otherwise an obedient, efficient bird-finder, you just might be better off to change your style of hunting slightly. For instance, maybe you should take up pheasant hunting in the Great Plains and get another dog which might be better suited to the grouse and woodcock coverts. Although all dogs can work nicely at a close range, some require more effort on the hunter's part to keep them there. Don't despair, though. As your dog ages, he'll learn what you want provided you insist on his staying in range, always.

Bolting

This is perhaps the most maddening fault of all and probably the inspiration for a long tirade of expletives, unpublishable and unfit for polite discourse. The bolting dog is a dog which refuses to come in when called. Such a dog will do whatever he wants and go where he pleases, regardless of his owner's threats of reprisal for this act of insubordination. In all probability the bolter will simply go into the field and become a confirmed self-hunter. This bad habit is reinforced each time he does it. Such a dog will eventually come back without any remorse over the torment, embarrassment, or hardship he may have caused his owner. If your dog bolts once and gets away with it, rest assured he'll do it again.

The best remedy for this problem is prevention. Don't give your dog the opportunity to run off on you. If you maintain constant control of your dog, he'll develop into a civilized obedient companion you'll be proud to call your own. If, however, you let him run on his own with no control over his direction or activities, he'll become a renegade. Act immediately the first time your dog bolts. Go back to heavy discipline and make your dog wear the spiked force collar and thirty or fifty-foot checkcord while out in the field. We could go one step further and let him don a shock collar as well. With all the hardware around his neck, he won't know what hit him when you shock him the next time he attempts to bolt. Provide him the opportunity to run off on you. When he does, make your reprimand fast and sure with a good dose of current so he understands that a command is a command and that you are the master he serves, not himself. If you correct his vice in a timely and thorough fashion, you can be sure your dog will not ruin a future hunting trip for you by bolting.

Photo 41 by: Len Jenkins.

This classy, though big-running pointer, owned by Jim Lance of Warren, Michigan, was effectively controlled by the spiked force collar. She was worked while dragging a short checkcord attached to her collar until she learned to be reasonable. This curbed out-of-gun-range casts and bird busting. This stunning pointer does it all and does it right!

Bumping

This fault is correctable provided your dog has a good nose, likes to point or flush (depending on whether he's a pointing or flushing dog), and wants to please. Bumping occurs when your dog inadvertently waltzes into birds which flush wild, surprising both the dog and the hunter. There are a number of things you can do to correct this problem:

- You can make the dog keep his head high, ensuring that he will more effectively smell birds. If he works with a low head, trailing the ground like a hound, he won't wind birds. Get his head high and help him keep it there by using your spiked force collar.

- You can always make sure you're working <u>into</u> the wind. If you cross a field with the wind to your back or obliquely at either side, there's a good chance you'll bump every bird in the field as your quartering dog runs right up on them, never smelling any. Work into the wind if you want your bird dog to find birds.

- You can go back to basics and insist on steady points a good distance from the bird. Insist on steady points in practice in which your dog holds point. If yours is a flushing dog, review his discipline so he doesn't run foolishly around the field without using his nose. You can tell when he's making game by the merry tail and animation. If a flushed bird surprises your dog, he's loafing, not working the birds as he should. Review your early training lessons with your flushing dog. A good gun dog doesn't lollygag; he works.

- You can slow your dog down if he overruns birds because he's too fast. Practice with him by going back to planted pigeons. Let him see that he'll find birds if he keeps his head high while working methodically at a <u>moderate</u> pace.

If your dog likes birds, we can easily correct him if he starts bumping his birds. He'll just have to learn to be more careful. With guidance from you, he'll learn this and also find out that care and precision pay off in terms of plenty of bird action, a situation preferable to accidental flushes.

Low Head And Low Tail

Bird dogs are elegant when they work, holding heads high and bounding methodically through coverts in an animated manner with cracking tails. If your dog carries his head low like a hound, he's far from elegant. In fact he's far from being an effective bird dog since he won't smell as many birds as a high-headed winding dog. If he shows signs of trailing body scent and putters around with head low, tug on his spiked force collar often. Also, plant lots of birds for him once you get him to keep his head up. He'll soon learn to hold his head high when he figures out that he smells more birds this way.

If he's got a low tail, you can help him a little by using a small saw blade when you have him on point. Each time he points, tap or stroke the underside of the tail with the serrated edge of the saw blade. While a dog naturally carries a higher point when extremely excited over birds, some don't get their tails up very high, although they're otherwise quite attractive on point. If yours is a low-tailed dog, just do your best. If you like high tails and haven't yet purchased a good gun dog prospect, seriously consider either an English setter or a pointer. The tails are beautiful. If you don't mind a low tail, that's what you'll probably get in the Irish and Gordon setters as well as the show-style English setters. If you have a short-tailed dog, don't worry much about tail carriage on point. There's more to a dog than just the tail.

Dropping Or Sitting On Point

This is an unattractive tendency in some dogs, perhaps going back to the primordial desire to creep up on game and then explode onto it in a sneak attack of sorts. This tendency, in fact, was a trait for which breeders selected in the early days of bird dog development prior to the advent of firearms. Well, we don't throw nets over birds anymore so let's do everything in our power to keep your gun dog standing tall and proud with ears cocked forward and head and tail held high. In order to get an elegant pointing stance, do everything possible by encouraging your dog to point with style. Do this during your training sessions, and he'll remember that you expect a stylish point out in the field.

If your dog crouches on point, stand him up while using a low mellow voice, repeating "*Whoa*" soothingly as you style him up. If he insists on dropping or crouching again, repeat the styling up process. The small saw blade might come in handy here. As your dog crouches, tap him lightly on his underside with the blade. In case he doesn't remain standing, you may need to replace your saw blade with one which has longer, sharper teeth. Just keep working on this problem, but don't get annoyed with your dog because he might detect your displeasure and associate it with his pointing the bird, not the low stance. With enough repetition, you should improve his style on point. You can have a stylish dog although your dog may never point exactly as you wish. Should this be the case, it might be time for you to accept what is and adjust your expectations. After all, if you don't like what you're looking at, you can change the way you look at it. Right? A low point, provided it's not too low, isn't that bad. Some things can't be changed completely. For example, modern setters are typically beautiful, stylish, high-tailed, and elegant on point. Yet they got the name *setter* in the early days of their development as a breed because they *set* low to the ground. If this primordial *setting* tendency is excessively strong in your dog and he is otherwise a fine bird dog, it's time for us to compromise a bit.

Catwalking

If your dog creeps in on a bird once point is established, he's catwalking. Catwalkers usually are very birdy dogs with an all-consuming desire to produce game. The only problem with this habit is that the catwalking dog will make the birds nervous; and they'll flush prematurely, probably before the hunter is ready to make the shot, and thereby cheating both dog and hunter out of much pleasure.

Catwalking is usually caused by an over-zealous trainer enticing a pup to creep in too close to a visible bird or bird wing when the pup is on point. The problem is further reinforced as long as the trainer permits and encourages the pup to creep in on birds in this manner. The catwalking is a flaw created by a trainer who allows the dog to take steps after being commanded *Whoa*. Well, *Whoa* means <u>*Whoa!*</u> Let's do

Photo 42 by: Bill Bolyard.

Mike's Magic Angel ,owned by Mike Jenkins, had a tendency to catwalk as a youngster. Mike effectively curbed this tendency with a spiked force collar. Angel holds a perfect point now!

something about catwalking when your pup initially shows this inclination. The first thing we can do is put the spiked force collar and checkcord back on and work the dog only while he's dragging his checkcord. If he shows signs of catwalking, jerk the checkcord and command *"Whoa!"* Do this in practice several times on planted pigeons. If he continues to show tendencies to catwalk, it's time for us to tackle this problem head-on so the dog doesn't ruin what should otherwise be good bird work. The following three strategies, used individually or in combination, should break the dog of catwalking:

- Walk (*Heel*) your dog up on the training table. Make him stand there when you say *"Whoa."* Review his basic discipline. By using the training table you'll keep your intense catwalking bird dog somewhat insecure and closer to your level because he's so far off the ground. Then produce a harnessed pigeon and place it on the training table. Make your dog hold point and prevent catwalking by applying pressure to the spiked force collar. Do this over and over again as necessary. If you can find an assistant to help you, you'll be able to do more. Once the dog stops catwalking on the ramp or top of the table, you can test him in the field again on planted birds. Until he's cured of his problem, however, do not take him out in the field on wild birds.

- Another way to prevent or cure catwalking is to take your dog into *Bird Dog Heaven*. If you have access to a pheasant flight pen with good flighty birds in it, take your dog inside (under restraint, of course). This is frustrating for him and it involves only sight pointing. While inside, review your early pointing lessons with your dog. Make him point the birds and hold his points. Use a commanding voice to *Whoa* him if he breaks point or catwalks and simultaneously apply pressure to your dog by jerking or pulling his checkcord and spiked force collar. This activity will put your dog into a hypnotic trance of sorts, and we can demonstrate for him repeatedly that he can enjoy this state if he holds a steady point. Since he won't be permitted to jump in on the birds or catwalk, he'll learn to enjoy having *possession* of his birds by holding them on point.

- If your dog still insists on catwalking, you can cure him with the electronic collar provided he already has had some experience with this device. (Refer to the next chapter.) We don't want your dog to associate the shock with the birds, but rather with catwalking (doing what he knows we don't want). Make sure your collar is set on low. We only want to tickle him a little with our electronic reminder. While most dogs can learn to break their bad habits with the collar attached in the usual location, let's not take any unnecessary chances with your dog's thinking that possibly the bird caused the *tickle*. Instead of placing the electronic collar on his neck, put it instead around his belly, making sure the collar points are in contact with the tender skin on his belly. When he gets the low electric stimulation, he'll associate it with walking in since it's coming from behind, not with the bird ahead of him.

Let's break your pointing dog of catwalking, using whichever method works. This is a completely correctable flaw. However, if your dog is a retriever or flushing spaniel that has a tendency to pursue game in a catwalking manner, keep encouraging him to continue. Flushers can sneak up on game and flush; pointers can't. Let's make sure your dog handles in a manner appropriate for his breed.

Excitement Over Frequent Bird Finds

This is a fault, but just think how much greater the fault would be if the dog didn't get excited! The problem with excessive excitement is that the dog starts running fast and wild, busting birds, and tearing out after them in a frenzied manner. You don't want a series of wild flushes with some maniac of a dog chasing from one extreme of the field to another going *bonkers* over every flushed bird. This is definitely not the manner of a gentleman's or lady's personal gun dog. Let your dog know that he is to find, point, or flush (depending on his breed) each bird in a civilized manner. Let him know that frenzy leads to chaos and an empty game bag.

If your dog goes crazy over frequent finds (large numbers of birds close together as one might find during the woodcock migration or on Pelee Island, Ontario's annual pheasant hunt), go back to square one and repeat some of the training techniques already cited with one serious modification. Instead of setting out one or two birds, set out many. Encourage your dog to find each one, making a great commotion over each with exaggerated praise. Yet after every flush, call the dog back with an authoritative, long *"don't mess up or else"* blast of the whistle, acknowledging every properly executed point or flush with lavish praise. Repeat the process loading the bird field with several birds to be found in rapid succession.

After each one, demand a call back for proper acknow-ledgment. Then send your dog out again for the next find. You call the shots, not the dog. Locating birds will thus be done enthusiastically, yet systematically. Wild, indis-criminate, maniacal flushes and bumps are not acceptable under any circumstances. Ours is a civilized sport--not for the obsessed--whether dog or human. There's a right way to do everything, and frenzy is never proper. After all, the rules of etiquette should be followed, even in the field.

False Pointing

An overly cautious dog will sometimes false point, usually while catwalking. The problem itself is easy to correct be-cause it shows that the dog is extremely interested in finding birds, almost to the point of its being an obsession. Such a dog doesn't want any birds to get away. He will continually sift the air currents, using his nose like a vacuum cleaner, and lock up on many successive points whenever he smells (or thinks he smells) birds. A false pointing dog is preferable to one that bumps his birds because the false pointer will follow-up all leads. In fact, sometimes he'll even point areas in hedge rows and other such places that just look *birdy*, breaking point and moving on when he realizes that no bird is present. Perhaps it's just wishful thinking, but at least the false pointer wants to produce game for the gun.

False pointing is usually caused by over-handling the dog in the early stages of training and/or by always setting birds out in the same locations each time. To break the dog of false pointing, give him plenty of experience on lots of planted birds. When he crosses the field and begins false pointing in places where you know there are no birds, urge him on until he goes on a hard point on a planted bird. Encourage him to

Whoa here. After the point is concluded and the planted bird is flushed or shot, urge him on to the next; but be sure to rush him whenever he false points. Don't indulge him by allowing him time to get his hopes up. With plenty of experience, resulting in actual bird finds, your false pointing dog will eventually become adept at only pointing birds, not just the locations where he wishes birds were hiding.

We must be very careful in *correcting* the false pointer since we don't want to make him careless. The best correction is to minimize the amount of time he can false point. Of course, you have to be judicious in this matter because sometimes wind currents will be unusually gusty, and your dog might indeed be picking up real scent from a distant bird. Time will cure this problem. Be thankful that your dog wants to point birds so fervently that he will not let the hint of bird presence go unchecked. A false pointer will become a first-class pointing dog with experience, which is, after all, the best teacher.

Flagging

A dog which wags his tail stiffly while on point is flagging. While some dogs lock up on hard points and flag as part of their pointing manner, most flag out of uncertainty or because they see the bird and realize that they can easily pounce on it. Some dogs will flag all their lives, and we won't be able to stop this because it's hereditary. You'll have to revise your expectations and accept this if yours is such a dog. If he does everything else right, the flagging won't be that objectionable if his points result in bird finds. But if your dog flags sometimes and holds a rigid tail other times, he's flagging due to uncertainty, not the constraints of heredity.

Most flagging is caused by improper handling during early training. If the handler makes planted birds too visible to the dog and does everything in a routine fashion, the dog might flag on point because he thinks everything is a set-up. If you see this happening, vary your training techniques and the locations at which you plant birds. However, if you find that the dog continues to flag, there is a remedy that usually works if adjustments in your timing and technique fail to bring about improvement.

This correction involves bringing the dog up on the training table and using the spiked force collar. Ask an assistant for help here because you'll need to concentrate on your dog. While you're heeling your dog away from the table, have your assistant place a harnessed bird on the training table. Turn your dog around and then walk him up the table. *Whoa* him firmly when he sees the bird. Because he's up off the ground and closer to your level, your dog will concentrate more in compensation for the insecurity he feels while on the table. This will necessarily cause his points to be more intense and stiff. When he's on point, stroke or tap the underside of his tail with the serrated edge of the saw blade. Communicate to your dog that this hard, rigid pointing stance with tail stiff is what you want. Remove or flush the bird. Walk the dog down the ramp and repeat this process a few more times and your problem should be solved.

As you resume planting birds in the field, try to keep them hidden from the dog's easy view. A word of caution is in order regarding a flagging dog: work your dog on well-hidden birds only on days when there's a good breeze. When you get him downwind of the bird, he'll be certain a bird is really there. Since flagging is usually caused by indecision and uncertainty, the strong breeze will let him know in no uncertain terms that a hidden bird is located upwind.

Photo 43 by: Charlene Jenkins.
Flagging can be curbed by making the dog point on the training table. John Toman demonstrates how to control flagging by using a saw blade on the underside of the dog's tail. Note Mike's intensity while pointing the bird in front of him!

Sulking

If your dog can't take correction without becoming sullen, you've got a soft dog. Some gun dogs become sullen and sulk after correction because their feelings get hurt easily. Yet others, with an equally intense desire to please, can take the correction and go on working. While some dogs are by nature soft, most sulkiness in bird dogs is caused by over-handling and abuse by human beings and not by any sort of innate personality defect in the dog. If your dog sulks after correction and becomes sullen and intimidated by your handling techniques, you had better modify your method before you have a basket case on your hands.

Keep all your interaction with the sulky dog positive, showing approval, encouragement, and acceptance at every opportunity. When your dog requires correction, do it in a quiet yet firm manner and immediately rebound with kindness and acceptance after the correction is made. You cannot get angry because dogs, being perceptive, intuitive animals, will sense the anger and internalize it, resulting in more sulkiness. If you have to correct a sullen dog, do it gently and do it in good spirits. If your dog can't take abuse, don't yell at him or strike him. Some dogs require harsh treatment for correction while others don't. If your dog is one that doesn't, always think before you act.

Your dog may require a gentle hand all his life. Your dog may revert to a sullen posture at any time in his life if he perceives a humiliating, demeaning, unaccepting tone in your voice and handling techniques. Be careful. A soft dog, while requiring kid glove treatment, could be a very devoted, dedicated companion who thrives on pleasing his owner in the field. Such a dog can be a superb bird-finding machine when basking in the glow of your approval or a neurotic wimp when he senses your rejection or contempt. Handle him right. Think of him as being marked, *fragile--handle with care.*

Mousing

If your young dog is bored because he's not finding game, he might *mouse* by scratching around for mice and voles. When you detect this, do something immediately to curb this unattractive activity. Always use your spiked force collar and checkcord in early training. When you see your dog working with head down, give a tug, thereby communicating to him that you want his head up to wind birds, not down to forage for disgusting little rodents. If he starts scratching the ground, give an authoritative tug and two toots to signal him on to worthy quarry. Don't indulge him in any way. If you had wanted a digging, trailing, burrowing dog, you would have bought a hound or terrier, not a pointing or flushing gun dog. Let him know, in no uncertain terms, that mice are taboo.

If you see that your young dog is showing mousing tendencies early in training, overload your bird field with harnessed pigeons or other game birds. Let him learn early in life the ecstatic joy of searching out birds, not rodents. Encourage him every step of the way, letting your dog know he is to ignore mice (and all furred game for that matter) and to pursue the scent of feathered game exclusively. Never let your dog construe your patience with him as acceptance for mousing. A lowered head and digging are the tell-tale signs of this obnoxious quest. Stop it immediately or you might find someday to your embarrassment and annoyance that your *bird dog* prefers mice to explosive South Dakota ringnecks!

Refusal To Retrieve

Gun dogs typically like to retrieve game which has fallen to the gun, particularly if they've been introduced to retrieving early in their training. However, sometimes things don't work out as they should, and a gun dog may become a reluctant retriever. You have to analyze your particular circumstances if your bird dog gets careless or recalcitrant in the retrieving department. The problem is usually fairly easy to correct although you'll have to work at it by being persistent, consistent, and insistent every step of the way.

If your dog retrieved satisfactorily in the early days of training, but shows reluctance now, your task will be to review your earlier retrieving lessons with one basic modification-- you'll have to demand a retrieve before going on to any other activity. In this way your dog will realize that a retrieve to hand is required before he can move on to other activities which he might find more enjoyable. Be sure to use a light-weight dummy, preferably a small soft canvas one, a corn cob wrapped with bird wings, or a soft pliable toy. We don't want your dog unhappy about having to pick up and carry an awkward or objectionable object. Insist that he hold the object in his mouth, placing it there while holding the back of his head and applying pressure on his lower jaw with your other hand to prevent him from dropping the dummy. While he's holding the object, command "*Hold.*" Then command him to *Give* while you extend your hand under his mouth to accept the dropped object. Do this several times in succession, always praising your dog when he drops the object yet remaining firm and serious throughout the rest of the lesson. Don't move on to anything else like field work because we want your dog to become singularly concerned with mastering the lesson at hand. After the lesson is complete, put him back in his kennel to think about what you're doing and what you expect. He'll look forward to his next contact with you in the manner typical of bird dogs. He'll soon realize that you expect him to hold the object in his mouth and drop it in your hand if this is what you make him do when you train him. If he does it satisfactorily, put him up again and repeat the process another time. After about the third session, your dog will be very eager to hold the object and drop it into your hand so that he might get to do other, more exciting things like running in the field, or doing other tasks that elicit your praise and approval. Before moving on, continue working on the retrieve by throwing the dummy out a few feet and sending the dog after it by commanding "*Fetch.*" If he's reluctant to pick it up, go toward him and deliberately place the object in his mouth, commanding him to "*Hold,*" then "*Give.*" You can't get impatient or communicate anything to the dog except your firm resolve that he will do this right or he won't do anything else until he does. Maintain a firm and serious demeanor throughout the training process. When he holds the object willingly and drops it on command, become very enthusiastic and affectionate toward him. He'll soon learn to hold and drop obligingly in order to evoke this more pleasant response from his owner. Never get angry with your dog or lose patience. Once you begin retraining for the retrieve you must continue until the dog's performance is satisfactory. Praise him extravagantly when he does things right yet remain a *stone face* throughout the rest of his training. By this time your dog is probably eager for more excitement. Give it to him; throw the dummy out further and command *"Fetch."* Preface this, however, by relaxing a bit and making a game of your throwing the object. Make him want to run after it and bring it back to you, thereby getting more praise and the opportunity to do this again. What fun! After all, it sure beats staying in the kennel, alone, with nothing to do but ponder what it will take to please his best buddy--you.

In succeeding lessons you should do whatever it takes to make your dog want to hold and give the dummy. Make it a game. Let him walk by your side with the dummy in his mouth. Make him beg you to throw the dummy out for him to retrieve. Because we've suspended most other training temporarily, he'll become both proficient and enthusiastic about *Fetch*, *Hold*, and *Give*. Once he begs to retrieve, increase the pleasure. Substitute a frozen quail or pigeon for the dummy. Let your dog romp around the field. Playfully tease him as you throw out the frozen bird--what an interesting surprise for your dog! Make him want to bound out to *Fetch*. He'll bring it back to you with tail wagging and that *let's do it again, Boss* look in his eyes. Let's oblige him. Let's do it again and again.

Graduation day from retrieving school is approaching. Take your dog out into the field and begin reviewing all the other things which he's been taught. It's been a long time since he's had this pleasure. Plant a bird. Shoot it. Command *"Fetch, Come, Give."* Show the dog that retrieving is part of hunting. It's fun and exciting, but just because it's fun doesn't mean it's an option--it's a requirement. Retrieving is something he'll have to do right. When he works the fields for hard-flying birds, you shoot them and he retrieves them. That's the way it's done.

Some dogs have a problem wanting to pick up dead or crippled birds when there are many live birds in the vicinity. These live birds tempt the dog to continue his pursuit of them rather than to search for a bird already brought down. A dog that gets excessively excited over frequent finds will sometimes compound his fault by also refusing to retrieve a shot bird because he's too busy racing across the field in his frenzy to send all the birds into wild flight. A dog which does this will invariably spoil the hunt when you're fortunate enough to get into heavy bird concentrations such as migrating woodcock or large and numerous quail coveys. If your dog shows signs of refusing to retrieve a downed bird when he knows there is another live bird nearby, you'll have to act as soon as possible in order to correct this fault. He has to be reminded that retrieving is not an option. His job is not finished until every downed bird is retrieved.

If your dog needs work in this area, set out several birds and work your dog into them. Be sure to keep him on a checkcord and spiked force collar in order to restrain him in case he goes wild on you. You would also be wise to refresh his memory by reviewing your retrieving exercises using either a frozen bird or corn cob wrapped with bird wings. Next, set out the birds in a manner appropriate for what you're trying to accomplish. You can use mechanically or electronically sprung launchers if you wish to have absolute control. If your dog has developed the habit of working loose birds more aggressively than confined ones, you should set out six or eight bobwhite or coturnix quail. These can be dizzied first to help assure that they'll stay in the vicinity of their release. Allow a few minutes to elapse to permit the birds to regain their equilibrium and move around without being frightened away. Then bring your dog in and demand proper execution of task. Demand a perfect point (or flush if he's a flushing dog). Make the shot, dropping the bird in front of him so he can mark its fall. Then demand a perfect retrieve, praising your dog in a spirited way each time the retrieve is made. Continue with your training, giving your dog every opportunity to systematically and methodically work, point, and retrieve each of the birds. He should be able to work properly on the real thing if he is forced to retrieve all of the birds which are located and shot in rapid succession during this retraining exercise. If you're still unsure of your dog, repeat this process. Practice makes perfect.

Force retrieving is an option available to you if all else fails. There are various force retrieving methods. One involves pinching and the other using the electronic collar. Although this is a remedy for refusal to retrieve, you should avoid its use except as a last resort. It's better to have the dog retrieve because he wants to, not as a pain-avoidance response. A gun dog should be happy and animated. Force retrieving is effective in many cases and can be implemented if necessary. If you feel insecure about using force methods, you may wish to consult someone experienced in these methods to help you force your dog to retrieve on command. While force retrieving does yield results, it sometimes results in a slavish dog who finds no joy in his work. The lack of joy manifests itself in the dog's appearance and way of going. It's best, usually, to train a dog to retrieve in accordance with the positive techniques outlined in this book. All dogs can be taught to retrieve and most enjoy it.

Hardmouth

This fault involves a dog's deliberately destroying or eating a bird which has been shot. This very objectionable fault is correctable and should be addressed as soon as it shows up. Don't be too quick to condemn your dog, however, for having a hardmouth. You can't expect birds to be retrieved with completely unruffled feathers nor could you expect your dog to retrieve a wildly flapping pheasant or mallard drake without chomping down hard to dispatch the bird. There are times when a dog has to get a little rough with the bird yet unnecessary mutilation of the bird must be stopped. All reprimands associated with hardmouth must be rational enough to prevent the dog from developing an aversion to downed birds yet strong enough to prevent destruction of them, rendering them unfit for the table.

If your dog shows signs of hardmouth, go back to basic retrieve training. Require your dog to retrieve dead pigeons which are thrown out for him in an enthusiastic manner. If he seems too hard on the bird, make him hold the bird in his mouth for two or three minutes at a time, cautioning him throughout the exercise to be gentle with it. If he mishandles the bird, make him stop. Heel the dog while letting him carry the bird. Continue playing the game, making him enjoy retrieving the bird and giving it up unmangled so you can toss it out again. After practicing this several times, take your dog out in the field and shoot several pigeons or quail over him. Concentrate on watching what he's doing as he retrieves. At the first sign of excessive mauling of the bird, caution him sternly and make him hold the bird gently in his mouth as was done during the practice exercises. If he handles these birds gently enough and continues to enjoy retrieving, you can be reasonably sure he'll handle wild birds the same way. Just be sure to allow your dog to enjoy retrieving and carrying birds. When he relinquishes the bird to hand, throw it out again and let him carry it. After all, since your dog works hard for the birds, allow him some time to savor the pleasures. You'll be able to put the bird into your game bag soon enough. Letting your dog enjoy the bird a few moments is a small price to pay for preventing hardmouth.

Pointing Dead

This fault may or may not be objectionable to you. A dog *points dead* when he points birds brought down by the gun rather than picking them up for the retrieve. Such a dog has learned his early lessons well because you've taught him that his lot in life is to pursue and point game but never to catch it. He will thus find the shot game, often marking its fall, and then point it.

If you want to break your dog of pointing dead, you'll have to let him know that it is permissible for him to catch game under certain circumstances. He first must find and point it without crowding. You, the hunter, make the flush, shoot the bird, and then command your dog to *"Fetch."* In order to get your dog accustomed to picking up the bird (only after this sequence of events) you're going to have to drill him on retrieving, starting with inanimate objects and then progressing to a corn cob wrapped in feathers or a frozen pigeon to be used as a retrieving dummy. Through practice and repetition, followed by praise after each proper retrieve, your dog will learn that mouthing, retrieving, and carrying birds is permissible when you command *"Fetch."* To introduce the element of gunfire serving as his cue to retrieve, we'll take several pigeons or quail out into the field, placing them in mechanical spring launchers or bird release harnesses. As you work the field, you'll encourage your dog to point each bird. Then flush it and urge him on to *Fetch* when he's excited over the bird's dropping right before his eyes after gunfire. If we succeed in getting retrieves here, your dog should be cured of pointing dead.

Each dog is an individual with unique strengths and defects. Fortunately, strengths can be enhanced and defects corrected. If your dog's only defect is pointing dead and if you're not making very rapid progress at bringing about an improvement, don't despair. Pointing dead is not without advantage. For instance, a dog which points dead won't be the kind of dog that busts birds. He probably won't bump them either since he's typically a very methodical worker. A dog who points dead usually has a finely tuned and inherently strong pointing instinct and great desire to relocate and re-establish points after marking falls.

In short, a dog who points dead will still locate your downed birds, but those which are only lightly hit might run off and be lost to your game bag. However, if the bird was soundly peppered with shot and relocated and repointed by your dog, you can always go to the dog and simply pick up the bird he's pointing. Your dog has done the hard part. The least you can do is compromise a bit by accepting this fault for the present by putting off complete retrieve training to a later date. A dog that points dead is still a pretty fine dog. Remember, if you don't like what you're looking at, change the way you're looking at it. That kind of puts pointing dead in a different perspective, doesn't it?

Photo 44 by: Len Jenkins.
Charlen's Clout (left), owned by the writer and Darcy, owned by Preston
Crabtree, have these Brown County, Indiana quail under control. Although both
Clout and Darcy retrieve to hand, pointing dead is almost as good as a point on
live birds.

Soft Points

A dog that points half-heartedly or uncertainly is
demonstrating *soft points*. Such a dog may very well develop
into an assertive gun dog but lacks apparent commitment and
intensity early in his development. He might show more fire
in his pointing style at a later time, but he needs patience and
understanding from the handler. A dog which is soft on point
is frequently an over-handled or sensitive dog that has become insecure. There seems to be a conflict in a dog like this
because actually he has pointing instinct and desire yet seems
reluctant to produce hard points for fear of making mistakes.
If your dog starts losing his staunchness and self-confidence,
do everything in your power to build him up emotionally.
Give him a lot of praise, acceptance, and encouragement.

You have to be patient in bringing him out of this or you might ruin him completely. Go easy and be satisfied with less progress. So what if it takes a little longer to train him? Many sensitive gun dogs have been reluctant, uncertain performers because of what they must perceive as threatening, excessive pressure. Take a gentle posture toward such a dog. Many owners have realized that their immediate expectations were too high and required adjustment. A soft pointing dog, accepted, nurtured, and rewarded, has often become a hard pointing dog full of fire and flash. The style and intensity had to be drawn out in an accepting manner. If you like your dog in spite of his being soft on point, give him a chance. Be satisfied with what he gives you while modifying your training strategy to accommodate his problem. The wait and the effort will be worth the reward as your dog comes into his own.

Chasing (not pointing) Birds

A pointing dog that just momentarily points and then charges into the bird, making it take flight and then chasing it, is committing a serious sin. This kind of a dog is busting birds and then chasing them out of the county. Something needs to be done with such a dog. The problem of busting birds was already addressed, and the techniques used to rectify that problem will work here. We have another problem, however, complicating busting. Chasing is an annoying fault often leading to more busting as the dog tears out after a flying bird. To correct a dog that does this, work on improving points, obeying commands, and handling at a close range. To correct a chasing dog, use the spiked force collar in combination with the electronic collar. (Please refer to the next chapter, *The Shock Collar*, for information on its proper use.) Reprimand the chaser for his offense by tugging forcefully on the checkcord and spiked force collar if he disobeys the whistle command to come (one long, authoritative, hard blast). Tempt the dog to chase a few times by letting birds fly after being released from mechanical spring launchers. Then let the dog relax a bit. After another find in which you make him point, repeat this process. If he chases, shock him. He'll come barrelling back to you and almost apologize for disregarding your whistle command to come back.

If you find that your chasing dog will not hold his point but rather insists on busting into the birds, you'll have to do something dramatic to break this pattern. Chances are that he will charge into the birds even though he's wearing the spiked forced collar. If that's the case, equip your chaser with an electronic collar set on *low*. If he takes steps or tries to charge into his birds, give him the light jolt, putting him on notice that this charging automatically results in moderate pain. If he's been shocked for some other offense by the higher intensity shock, your light jolt will remind him that a more severe consequence just might be eminent. He'll probably shape up in a hurry. Practice until you break his unacceptable pattern of chasing birds instead of pointing them. Chasing just won't do, except if he's a flushing dog.

Breaking Point

If your dog breaks point prematurely and prevents you from flushing the bird, you've got a dog that has the rules mixed up. Set that dog straight. The hunter flushes, not the dog. There are some hunters who train their dogs to flush the quarry but only after the hunter gets in position for a shot. If you like this method, that's fine. It's especially effective if your dog is used for pheasants. However, if your dog simply rushes in and breaks into birds without waiting for you, he's cheating you. You'll have to reinforce your early training by using your spiked force collar. Ask a friend to assist you by stepping on or grabbing the checkcord your dog is dragging. This will prevent your dog from breaking point as you advance toward the bird. Look back at the dog and command "*Whoa*." Make sure this involves eye contact for maximum impact. Flush the bird and shoot. Send the dog out for the retrieve as your assistant releases the checkcord. Repeat this a few more times to establish in the dog's mind that it is you who flushes the birds. He must be taught that there is no action unless the hunter initiates it. If your dog refuses to accept this, perhaps a little electricity will help him see things your way. (Please refer to the next chapter, *The Shock Collar*, before using this training device.) If you decide to use the electronic collar to persuade him, set it on low (never shock severely around birds). Your dog will get the picture after a little stimulation.

Deer Running

If you hunt in deer country, there's a good chance your dog will cave in to temptation and temporarily forget everything you've taught him when a deer suddenly catches his eye. If this happens once, you'll have to make sure it doesn't happen again. A dog running deer is an out-of-control dog who is ruining your hunt, running the risk of getting lost for a long time, and jeopardizing his own life as he forgets all caution in his quest of deer. The best thing you can do with a young dog is to take him into an area containing deer prior to a real hunt. Provide him with exposure to deer and reprimand firmly with "*No*" if he shows interest in chasing deer. Initiate this exposure by keeping your dog under tight control. Don't let him loosen up. Keep him preoccupied with your control by reviewing basic discipline. The best thing that could happen is for him to find a deer and be commanded "*No!*," thus communicating to him in clear terms that he is to ignore deer or else face your anger.

If you're hunting grouse, you're hunting in deer country. You can minimize your dog's inadvertent distraction with deer if you keep the dog belled. The tingling noise will keep you aware of the dog's location while it alerts the deer of your dog's presence, thereby giving them ample opportunity to evade the dog's notice well in advance of his approach.

If your dog does run deer and refuses to give it up easily, the electronic collar can be used effectively. (Refer to the next chapter, *The Shock Collar*, for further information.) If your dog chases a deer, command "*No!*" and then administer the shock. Your dog will think the deer caused the pain and he'll desist from his chase. You'll do yourself and your dog a big favor by breaking him of running deer, an activity which is illegal and dangerous as well as very unbecoming for a bird dog. Deer are taboo.

Nuisance Barking

If your dog barks incessantly, he's either bored or is trying to get your attention. Because you can't keep him entertained every minute, your dog is going to have to learn to cope with boredom. As far as attracting your attention is concerned, make sure he realizes that the attention attracted is most unpleasant. Unless you like sleepless nights or irate neighbors, a barking dog is not to be tolerated.

In the event that your dog won't quit barking, try to find out if there's a problem. For instance, his kennel area could be frequented by nocturnal guests such as raccoons, cats, or rodents. If this happens, you should try to get rid of whatever is attracting the visitor. Usually it's the food so don't leave his food out at night. If the dog persists in barking for no reason other than to beg you to let him come in for company, you can stop this very easily by using one of the no-bark trainers. This handy device has a sensor which is activated by the vibration of the dog's vocal chords.

As the dog barks, the vibration causes a swift, sure emphatic shock. Your dog's bad habit will be corrected quickly without your having to punish him. You'll be able to enjoy a quiet environment after your dog receives a couple of jolts. Peace at last!

Most faults caused in a dog are man-made. Dogs are not born gun-shy, for instance. They're made that way.

17

The Shock Collar

The essential premise woven throughout the fabric of this book is that your dog will develop into a fine gun dog provided you train him effectively through consistent techniques administered by a firm yet kind hand. Nowhere is physical abuse advocated as a means of developing a gun dog. However, there may be times that an untrained or very spoiled older dog may require a good shaking or cuffing because he's already learned that he can disregard commands with impunity. Since each dog is an individual, the techniques used must be tailored to the particular dog and his unique needs. Physical abuse is a technique of last resort and should never be used as a matter of course. Firm methods and manner using the restraint imposed by the spiked force collar and checkcord constitute the strategy of choice. Should your methods or tools not bring about the desired results, however, the electronic trainer, more commonly referred to as the *shock collar* or *electric collar*, can quickly bring about a positive change if used sensibly. Don't rule out this device. It has many applications and advantages if used properly and sparingly.

The main advantage of using the collar is that you can administer sure, swift punishment for misconduct or disregard of commands by simply pressing the transmitter button. If you do it right, the your will associate the electrical jolt with his misconduct or disobedience rather than with you. In this way you can correct misbehavior in a timely fashion, stopping it before it becomes firmly entrenched in your dog's mode of working. There will be no need for striking your dog or chasing him down, two old methods of correction which often backfire. Another advantage of the shock collar is that the dog is required to exercise free choice. He can decide if he wants to obey a command or modify a behavior, or he can decide to ignore what is being expected of him. If the collar is used, he will quickly learn that commands are commands and that the best decision on his part is compliance. On the other hand, if the electric collar is not used, the dog may learn that he can choose whether to obey or not, depending upon how he feels about it or his natural inclinations. If he chooses to disregard the command, he knows there's nothing his owner can do about it. The owner may get angry but he'll still accept the dog and soon forget about the misconduct. Dogs are smart. They know when you can impose restraint and when you can't. The electronic collar allows you to establish in the dog's mind that you are indeed the one in control and that your expectations are to be realized unequivocally.

Your training methods should be done by conventional or traditional means in the beginning. The shock collar is _not_ a substitute for these methods. The dog must be taught what you want by using the basic tools first. If you find that your dog starts developing bad habits in spite of the effort you've already expended through traditional training, the electronic collar should be considered. It is not unkind. It does allow the dog to make the right decision. It delivers immediate results. Since you've already done your homework with your dog and established a good relationship with him, the shock collar can be used effectively.

The electronic collar can be used in combination with your spiked force collar. Allow the dog to work with both collars on. Tug on the checkcord and spiked force collar for correction as you've done previously. Give the dog every opportunity to revert to his bad habit. When he does, press the transmitter button and send him a message. If his problem was non-compliance with a whistle command, for instance, he'll think twice about ignoring the whistle in the future. If he was trying to do something you don't allow like running deer or digging for mice, he'll think these furred animals magically zapped him, not you. Give your dog more opportunities to make the right decision. Let him learn that the incorrect decision results in a shock.

All dogs react to the shock but they react differently. Your dog may run to you for comfort if you've already established in his mind that you're a source of security. This is good. He'll mostly stay at your feet for a while. Don't get annoyed at this. It's temporary. He'll go out and work again once he relaxes. Some dogs run away to hide when shocked. If your dog tries this, make sure you don't allow him to succeed. Be quick after shocking and grab the checkcord. Call him to you enthusiastically in a consoling manner. After all, you didn't punish him; the act of disobedience did. You're still his friend, the one he wants to please.

Try to use some finesse when putting the electronic collar on your dog. Play with him a lot and make sure your communication with him is enthusiastic. First, put on the spiked force collar. Tug around his neck, ruffing him up a bit in a playful way. Then put on the shock collar below the spiked force collar in a discreet manner. Since a well-trained dog won't require much shocking (perhaps only two or three times), you'll want him to be confused as to which piece of hardware around his neck may have caused the shock. Keep him unsure of this. Do everything in your power to prevent your dog from becoming *collar wise*. You can do this in a variety of ways once you analyze what your dog's problem is and decide on a method for correction. A dummy collar, having about the same weight and feel as the real thing, should be used first. Of course, there won't be a shock. Then discretely change collars. Once you think your dog's problem is cured, you can run him with the dummy collar and spiked forced collar with checkcord dragging. Next use the spiked forced collar and checkcord. Graduate to just the dummy, and finally only his standard nylon or leather every-day collar. You'll be pleased that the electronic collar allowed you to correct your dog's problem. You'll even be more pleased with yourself knowing that you did the correction in an intelligent manner to prevent the dog from becoming *collar wise*.

Don't use the shock collar to excess. If a light shock on the low setting will do the job, use low. If one or two shocks for correction are sufficient, don't use more. If your dog can't take correction easily, be very conservative with the collar. Use it wisely and sparingly in a timely manner.

There are a variety of uses for the electronic collar:

- The shock collar can be used in combination with the spiked force collar and checkcord to correct the dog when he disregards the whistle.

- The shock collar will cure your dog of chasing undesirable animals like rabbits, cats, deer, mice, or songbirds.

- The shock collar is effective in breaking bad habits such as chasing automobiles and bicyclists. Set up a situation in which a friend tempts your dog to chase. When the dog gives in to temptation, command "*No!*" If he doesn't stop, deliver the current.

- The shock collar set on low can fine tune your dog in advanced yard training. The dog will become very preoccupied with not making mistakes. Although the collar will help speed the training process, it's always best to yard train by traditional means.

- The shock collar should not be used when the dog is around birds in the early stages of bird contact. You don't want a bird dog to conclude that the bird caused him to get shocked! Bird-shyness could result very easily if you're not judicious in the use of the collar around birds. There are times, however, when the collar will help correct a problem such as bumping, chasing, or catwalking. Make sure that your dog has had ample bird contact without having the shock administered. You can use the collar around the dog's neck in the usual position or you can put it around his midsection so as to administer the shock to his belly. This is useful in curbing catwalking, for instance, because the dog will think the shock was caused by his taking steps (behind) and not by the bird (in front). Make sure you're careful in the use of the collar when your dog is around birds. Keep your stimulation intensity on low and as brief as possible.

- The shock collar, coupled with a firm hand, may help you civilize an outlaw dog.

- A shock collar can be used to curb nuisance barking. Shock the dog when he barks unnecessarily.

Photo 45 by: Dan Wizner.

Riley, an English setter owned by young Tom Colthurst of Saginaw, Michigan, waits with anticipation to begin hunting grouse in the Tittabawassee. The conservative, judicious use of electric current helped to channel the energy of this exuberant setter. Riley handled both grouse and pheasants like a veteran during her first season. The collar, wisely used, was a factor.

The electronic collar is a useful tool when properly used. It's _not_ a substitute for the practice of sound training techniques. In spite of administering a somewhat painful shock, the electronic collar is a humane training tool when used sensibly. It eliminates or minimizes the need for physical reprimand while allowing the dog to concentrate on executing his lessons in the proper manner. The choice is his. He can choose what's right or what's wrong, knowing that if he opts for the wrong response an electrical message will mysteriously advise him that he made the wrong decision and that he must not do it again. Since he knows you're always there to praise him for the right decision, you'll maintain a good rapport with him which in turn will guarantee his acceptance of your training methods.

Don't rule out the use of the electronic collar, but by the same token don't become dependent on it by skipping essential steps in traditional training. This is the age of technology, and you have a useful tool at your disposal in case you need it. Just use it wisely and humanely.

Training is like a jigsaw puzzle. You complete the puzzle one piece at a time.

18

Dealing With Shyness

Good gun dogs are typically aggressive in the field, but some are rather shy otherwise. This is really not a fault in general, but rather just the nature of some individuals. A shy dog can be a very useful, productive dog. You as the owner must be careful in handling your dog if he demonstrates tendencies toward shyness.

While most shyness is caused by inadequate socialization as a pup, problems can arise at any time during the dog's life. A gun dog is a working dog who thrives on acceptance by his master. He wants to please. Sometimes he might detect that he's not gaining your approval and, consequently, your love. Be careful with such a dog so you don't cause sullenness. Be patient in your handling and conscious of your impact on your dog so you don't make him withdraw.

Timidity is sometimes cited as a problem with some dogs. If your dog is becoming increasingly timid, try to analyze

Photo 46 by: Preston Crabtree.

A pasel of puppies. These English setters are good ones, but inproper handling could cause shyness. Treat pups sensibly and avoid the problem of shyness.

Photo 47 by: Dan Wizner.

Vivian DeRiemaker introduces her Chesapeake Bay retriever, Zack, to Charlen's Bill Crockett at one of the writer's training clinics at his Tittabawassee Forest grounds. Socialization is very important.

what's going on. Even though some dogs have a propensity for boldness and some for timidity, extreme timidity to the point of the dog's fear of everything is caused by human beings. Think about what you're doing. Don't ruin a sensitive dog by a blustering manner. You can have a fine, easily managed, stylish gun dog if you exercise restraint and patience in your handling and training. A sensitive dog that loves his master is a dog who wants to please. Capitalize on this desire and you'll have a dog who will give his all for you.

Some dogs feel very secure when they're in their homes or in the field alone with their owners. They will, however, show signs of timidity when other people or dogs are around. This, of course, can be a problem if you decide to hunt with a group of friends or to enter your dog in a field trial or hunting test. In order to prevent this kind of behavior, give your dog lots of social experience. You can do any of the following things to get your dog to accept the fact that life is varied and full of change:

- Take him for walks downtown.
- Take him out in the field with another dog with which he is familiar.
- Enroll him in a dog obedience class.
- Take him with you for rides in the car.
- Take him to places where he can witness much commotion and excitement.
- Introduce him to friendly new people and dogs.

If your dog learns to accept new experiences, new people, and new dogs, he should overcome any inclination toward shyness. Let him learn that life is full of change but that change and uncertainty are not in themselves a threat to his well-being. Be patient with a shy dog, and you'll be gratified with his devotion to you, the source of his feelings of security and acceptance.

> *Don't cop out by blaming your dog, his breeding, the previous owner, or breed for problems unless you've first analyzed yourself, your techniques, your attitude, and your expectations.*

19

Shooting Preserves

Once your dog is trained, you'll want to give him some
practice handling birds under simulated hunting
conditions. A good way to do this is to take him to a shooting
preserve and have several birds set out. Because you'll want
to give your dog plenty of experience in all phases of bird work
(including the retrieve), you may wish to ask a friend to come
with you. Besides providing ample experience for your dog,
you'll be able to split the expenses, perhaps double the action,
and have a back-up gun to ensure that all birds are brought
down for your dog. In addition to putting into practice everything you've taught your dog, you'll have a good time.

Shooting preserves can offer quality shooting. Many have
wonderfully maintained grounds containing good habitat and
food plantings of sorghum and other grains. If the stocked
pheasants, quail, or chukars are fully mature well-conditioned
birds accustomed to flying in a flight pen, you'll be in for some

Photo 48 by: Valrie Lewis.
Gordon Lewis enjoys another day afield at Vermont's Tinmouth Shooting Preserve.

Photo 49 by: Dan Dishong.
Hard-flying ringnecks provide challenging sport at Ringneck Ridge Hunting Club, Gibsonburg, Ohio.

Photo 50 by: Dick Geswein.
A pair of performers pointing quail at the licensed shooting grounds of Buckeye Kennels, Waterloo, Ohio.

fast, furious sport which could even rival wild hunting. Although the birds may be a little slower, there is a great benefit to your dog in the number of consecutive birds which he can handle and which you can bring down for the retrieve. Even one experience at a shooting preserve can make a difference as far as getting your dog ready for hunting completely wild birds. You might like it well enough to join the club, guaranteeing yourself and your dog plenty of action for a much longer period of time than the standard open season on wild birds. Look into going to a preserve. Try it at least once to see if you like it.

Read your dog's body language.
He's reading yours!

20

Beauty--More Than Skin Deep

Think about what it takes for a dog to be a great hunting partner. Markings, gender, and color, profuse feathering, and extreme adherence to show conformation standards mean absolutely nothing to the upland hunter who appreciates the beauty, skill, and grace inherent in a fine gun dog. The hunter looks for traits such as innate intelligence, stamina, hunting instinct, drive, desire, animation, a merry way-of-going, and companionability. If a dog has these qualities, the beauty requirement so many of us seek is adequately met. The dog in action is sheer beauty, a living piece of art to be treasured and enjoyed. The success achieved at the end of the hunt in either bagged game or personal satisfaction attests to the dog's qualities. In short, a good dog is a good dog, regardless of physical characteristics as observed when he is <u>not</u> hunting.

In order to possess a good (or great) hunting dog, don't get preoccupied with cosmetic characteristics. If you want a show dog, get one. If you want a hunting dog, select appropriately. For the field, you want an athlete, a rugged, durable individual who will work hard for you. He should be a performance dog who takes both pride and pleasure in his work. You want a dog with the spirit to love a good game, one who is up to meeting any challenge physically, mentally, and strategically while doing so in accordance with rigorous rules of etiquette. You want an intelligent animal. You want a dog bred over the generations to perform in a very intricate way by coordinating his inherent instinct and knowledge of wild bird habits with your very sophisticated rules in a way that satisfies you. Show dogs won't cut it in this regard because they were most likely bred to primarily conform to a show standard. Usually they are lack-luster in the field because hunting performance was not used in the culling process over the generations.

Edward J. Volk

Photo 51 by: Len Jenkins.
Kate, a young English setter pup owned by John Karpinski of Detroit, Michigan, knows what she wants. The desire has been bred in!

Performance requirements weed out the unfit. Therefore, those individuals with intelligence, naturally suitable dispositions, stamina, structural strength and nose contribute their qualities to the gene pool when selectively bred. Natural ability breeds on. If you select your dog from accomplished ancestors, you have the advantage of getting a dog whose progenitors were bred together because of their field sense. If you select a pup from show breeding in which field performance was not stressed, you will probably end up with an inadequate gun dog.

Don't shy away from dogs of field trial background. The trials are largely responsible for the upgrading of field dogs over the years. The most competitive, hard-working, stylish, birdy dogs must vie with one another for top honors. The winners have met the most demanding tests and have proven themselves. These winners contribute immensely to the improvement and development of our sporting breeds. In general, the best, bred to the best, produce the best. A dog incorporating the blood of field trial winners as well as accomplished gun dogs is bound to be your best bet if you are looking for a dog to work the coverts and fields in quest of your favorite game. Such a dog, provided he has a cooperative disposition, is bound to be *field smart*. He may not meet the show standard, but he will be truly exquisite and elegant when and where it matters. He will be a sight to behold, the ultimate in beauty, brains, and brawn all fused into one for the sportsman's pleasure. That which is functional is inherently beautiful. And isn't beauty really in the *eye of the beholder* anyway?

A good dog is a good dog. Breed, color, gender, and markings are irrelevant.

21

Do You Like Your Dog?

Have you ever detected that someone doesn't like you? Or, have you ever found that you don't like another person--like a neighbor, co-worker, or business associate? Of course, nothing productive ever comes out of expressing your dislike for another or their expressing annoyance, disdain, or contempt for you. Yet the negative inclinations still exist and surface subtly from time to time. This negative thought is a real impediment to full cooperation and happiness. The same problem exists between you and your dog. If he doesn't like or trust you and if you really don't like him, you've both got problems. It is fundamental to training your dog that you like him as an individual. If you don't, maybe you should find him a new home because you will probably ruin him by your attitude. There is a good chance that another person will like and accept him, thereby getting the best from him.

Attitude Is Always A Factor In Training

You have your own faults. Your dog has his. Perhaps you need to make some adjustments regarding what is acceptable or desirable. In the case of dogs, or anything else for that matter, if you don't like what you are looking at, you can change the way you look at it. If you cannot correct your dog's conduct, manner or demeanor, you should reevaluate the situation. Perhaps the dog doesn't have a problem--you have. For instance, if your dog doesn't want to come when called, there's a good chance you caused the problem by not being assertive or consistent in your training, or you have never taken the time to develop rapport with your dog prior to the start of training. In other words, you are at fault and in order to correct your dog's annoying fault, you will have to correct your own first. Think about what you don't like about your dog and then analyze your own methods and manner. There just might be a correlation. Knowing that, you could do something about the problem. If you correct the problem, you just might like your dog more, thereby leading to greater success and satisfaction in training. The problem which you were initially looking at can be rectified with a change in the way you look at it. This just might lead to constructive resolution of a fault in both dog and master.

> *A little bit of praise at the right time will give your dog the feedback he needs for continued progress.*

22

A Written Program, Schedule, And Evaluation

Your training will be more effective if you have a definite plan of action, a time frame in which to achieve your goals, and an evaluative tool by which to gauge progress. Your plan can be firmly understood in the incipient days of training yet become elusive and ambiguous later on. In order to make sure you succeed, try committing your individual training program to writing when you begin the process. By reviewing this program, you will know you're on the road to accomplishing your mission--owning a finished gun dog. In order to facilitate realization of this program, you should incorporate a tentative time schedule into your agenda. This schedule should be tailored to each individual dog. There are many variables including your dog's age, his prior training, your expertise, and the dog's natural ability, inclination, and temperament. When you think you're finished, subject the results to evaluation to help measure your success. If you have a clear plan, you'll keep on course. If you don't articulate where you're going, you are likely to get lost. Check your written plan of action from time to time and assess accomplishment of your goals within your time frame. Then evaluate. The two evaluation checklists in this chapter are used in our training clinics and seem to work. One is a *Progress Report* for your dog while the other is a *Self-Evaluation*. You're the one who has to be satisfied. How are you doing?

There is no progress without incentive!

English Setters
Len Jenkins Custom Gun Dog Training Services
3260 Sheick Road, Monroe, MI 48161

Progress Report For _____

Does my dog:

☐ *Heel?*

☐ *Come* when called?

☐ Turn and/or go forward when directed (quartering)?

☐ Understand both whistle signals?

☐ *Whoa?*

☐ *Point?*

☐ Retrieve on command (*Fetch*)?

☐ Release retrieved object to hand (*Give*)?

☐ Keep his head up in order to wind birds?

☐ Show enthusiasm and animation when working?

☐ Keep his mind on task in spite of distractions?

☐ Behave in a mannerly way in general?

☐ Accept gun report without fear?

☐ Know the word *Bird?*

☐ Avoid chasing cars on road?

☐ Stop what he is doing, when so commanded (*No*)?

☐ Search for a downed bird (*Dead*)?

☐ Go to his quarters when told (*Kennel*)?

If most of your answers are "yes," you and your dog are doing well!

English Setters
Len Jenkins Custom Gun Dog Training Services
3260 Sheick Road, Monroe, MI 48161

Self-Evaluation For Owner:

- [ ] Do I like my dog?
- [ ] Do I set realistic goals?
- [ ] Am I consistent?
- [ ] Do I use only one clear word or signal for each command?
- [ ] Do I praise my dog?
- [ ] Do I analyze the training process to teach him one command at a time?
- [ ] Do I avoid giving commands I am in no position to enforce?
- [ ] Do I refrain from physical abuse?
- [ ] Do I control the dog or does he control me?
- [ ] Do I expect my dog to *heel, come* when called, quarter, and walk on the lead in a civilized manner?
- [ ] Do I expect good performance or am I satisfied with a sloppy execution of task?
- [ ] Do I value wildlife enough to expect my dog to retrieve all wounded game?
- [ ] Do I avoid giving my dog unrestrained freedom, thereby avoiding bad habits?
- [ ] Do I avoid letting my dog run around the fields without my being there, encouraging him to become a *self-hunter*.

☐ Am I persistent about correcting faults and optimistic about progress?

☐ Do I avoid *fooling* my dog unnecessarily?

☐ Do I expect my dog to be animated and enthusiastic?

☐ Do I really believe my dog will learn what he does, whether it is good or bad?

☐ Do I believe there is a proper etiquette in hunting with a gun dog?

☐ When hunting or working my dog, do I work into the wind?

23

Weather Or Not

Once you begin the formal training of your gun dog, it is very important to keep to a schedule. While formal training sessions need not be lengthy, they should be frequent. Even a ten minute session in which you simply review what your dog already knows is valuable in that it reinforces the notion that his mission in life is to work for you in order to gain your acceptance, approval, and attention. When it is time to advance to a more intricate task, you must plan the method and time for this and then work your plan. In case you don't succeed in your time allotment, be prepared to continue anyway so that you can end on a successful, happy note. If you have problems getting him to execute the new task, review what he already knows. Never put your dog away when you're angry or unhappy because of his failure to learn. He will just brood about it, and the sullenness which might develop will be an impediment to future sessions.

Photo 52 by: Eve Bryson.
If you want an excuse for not training, blame the weather. If it's too hot, dress accordingly. Work in the shade and provide your dog plenty of fresh water. The writer is working his pup, Chelsea, on the training table in the shade of apple trees.

Because your personal schedule is busy and extra time is a commodity in short supply, you may find that you would prefer not training. Well, take the time anyway. Just remember the paradox that you never have enough time, but you have all there is. Take the time--the rewards are worth it.

Besides the shortness of sufficient time, you may also find other obstacles to keeping on schedule. The most frequent problem is weather. Like things in general, nothing is ever exactly right, or at least to your unconditional, absolute liking. This includes the weather. It might to too hot, too cold, too windy, too still, too wet, too dry, or too humid. While you can't train in a blinding snowstorm or pounding downpour of rain or hail, the weather is usually tolerable. Train accordingly, and don't put off the training which needs to be done. If you

Photo 53 by: Jon Charles Anderson.
These gentlemen didn't let the freezing December rain deter them from training! Ray Brimm, of Romeo, Michigan and Bob Moriarty and Joseph Faucher of Utica, Michigan steady Lady, Blue, and Max, respectively, while the writer teases with a netted pigeon.

do, you might find yourself as well as your dog unprepared for the hunting season.

We all deal with many other demands on our time like family, jobs, and errands. With all life's frustrations, you just might find that a few moments daily with your loving, trusting dog will give you the strength and purpose needed to fulfill other obligations. The training can be your *therapy*, an activity in which you reap the rewards of satisfaction with yourself as well as your dog. The experience may help you mentally in meeting all your other obligations. You will also have the refreshing pleasure of working out-of-doors and doing something physical, ridding your mind and body of some of life's nagging frustrations and stress. The training may be as good for you as it is for your dog.

If you keep to your own schedule, you will have a well-trained gun dog. If you don't really want to train, you will always be able to find excuses. If you want a developed, stylish gun dog, no excuses, please!

If you want an excuse, you'll find one.

24

Buying An Older Dog

Although many hunters have the idea that they can save time and energy by starting with an older dog, there is no shortcut to effective gun dog training. They claim that they don't want to go through the trouble of raising and training a pup. It's really too bad they feel that way because they are cheating themselves out of a rewarding experience through which they could develop a truly personal gun dog. The relationship between the hunter and his dog is a special one indeed. A young, impressionable pup can learn at a very early age that he and his owner are a team. The owner is almost like a deity, and the pup will soon realize that his whole experience revolves around a very special relationship in which his new owner provides love, security, and field experience, that brings pleasure to both. The bonding which occurs at this time will facilitate all subsequent training. The young pup will learn that his mission in life is to please his owner in order to preserve the special bond between them.

Nonetheless, there are sportsmen who will forego the cementing of this special relationship because they want a dog to hunt for them _now_. If you are such an individual, you may find a suitable _started_ or _finished dog_ and establish a solid rapport with that dog provided you get to know him and build a working relationship. You must remember that a dog is a loving, devoted companion, not a machine. Even with an older _started_ or _finished_ gun dog, you still have to work on the relationship necessary to meld dog and hunter into a team.

There are many older pups available so finding one is no problem. Check sporting magazine classified sections or your local newspaper and you will most likely find a prospect. Some may have been well cared for household pets which now must go to a new home because of a change in their owner's circumstances. If you find such a dog, you will have to establish your own relationship with him and build on that which his previous owner has begun. Such a dog, provided he comes from good gun dog stock, is a suitable prospect because he has already learned at an early age to love and please his owner. Just hope he hasn't developed any vices. You can also find a satisfactory prospect from reputable breeders and trainers who have started training with the intention of selling the dog as a started or trained dog. If he was trained carefully through love and approval and not permitted to develop vices such as running off when called, blinking, or bolting, he's probably a good choice. With some effort, you could make something of him. Such a dog is valuable because special effort went into developing him. If the trainer treated the dog as he would his personal dog, you will find that you will be able to step in and replace the trainer as the dog's master. But this takes time.

A dog trained this way is valuable so be prepared to pay a fair price. You get what you pay for.

There are also many *started* or *trained* dogs available. These are sometimes the ones who were rejected as puppy prospects, ruined through inept training, abused or neglected in puppyhood, or in some other way damaged during the formative months in which they should have been developing a sound relationship with human beings. These dogs are usually very inexpensive. If you buy one which you want to hunt, you are still going to have to work with him. In fact, you will probably have to do a lot of re-training and correction in the process as such a dog, ironically, may require more time and skill on your part than a pup would. These older dogs can be trained and salvaged, and you're to be commended for undertaking such a task. Just don't be surprised if the dog isn't ready to hunt as soon as you had hoped. There is no substitute for the time necessary to make a dog yours. You'll have to put in the time if you want something good to come from your efforts.

In spite of obstacles and price, it is possible to start with an older dog and develop him into a suitable gun dog. If you decide to go this route, there are certain things which you should know. First of all, is the person selling the dog a person of integrity? If so, look into the matter further. Get to know the dog. Do you like him? Does he seem to like you? Don't start with a dog you don't like because your training will probably result in disaster. If you like the dog, ask the seller to show you everything the dog knows and does. See if the dog comes when called. Are there any special hand, voice, or whistle signals you should use in handling this dog? Take the time to work with the trainer so that you will know what the dog knows. If you're satisfied with what you have seen so far, ask the seller if you can fire a gun around the dog to make sure he isn't gun-shy. Ask to see the dog's reaction to birds. If you like everything you've seen in the dog, seriously consider him provided you don't plan on hunting him a week later. Remember the importance of time.

Before you buy the dog, make sure you understand the terms of sale. If there's any guarantee, have it in writing in order to prevent problems later because of implied understanding. If the dog is free of infectious disease, worm infestation, heartworm, and chronic ailments, you should take him if you like him. But if the seller tells you there's a serious health problem, you might wish to reconsider. Find out if the dog's immunizations are current because you'll want to have him properly vaccinated and licensed once you are legally responsible for this.

If the seller tells you that the dog doesn't know anything, don't rule out the dog. That's better than a dog who has developed bad habits. If you're told the older dog has be-

Photo 54 by Dan Wizner.

Charlen's Smokey is a superb Michigan grouse dog who comes from a predominantly southern background. The bloodlines of Johnny Crockett, Flaming Star, and Mr. Thor were combined with the Michigan-bred Ghost Train line to produce this dog.

havioral or health problems, you still might be able to bring him around through time. If you are willing to accept limitations and feel fully apprised of the dog's strengths and weaknesses, go ahead and consider the older dog. But if you want to start fresh, with no handicap, opt for a pup. If you truly love bird dogs and want the satisfaction of developing your own special, personal dog, it's best to start with a pup. In the long run, there's no shortcut.

> *If you and your dog don't really like each other, you've got problems.*

25

Grouse Dogs

A good bird dog should be able to hunt any game bird satisfactorily. Most hunters frequently hunt a variety of game birds so they expect their dogs to adapt accordingly. Each game bird species has its unique qualities and a gun dog will become proficient at working that particular species as he gains experience. While all gun dogs will work all game birds, the dog becomes a specialist depending on what is usually hunted. If you're a grouse hunter, though, you're going to want a dog with special natural inclinations and temperament for handling this particular bird. All gun dogs will hunt grouse, but they won't all do it well unless they've had the right training and experience. If they lack the right natural inclinations, you'll have a hard time training them and providing this experience.

A grouse dog must be well disciplined. Such a dog must handle easily in very heavy, rough cover. An out-of-control dog racing across the woodlands won't do in this regard because he'll just flush the grouse, making them unavailable for a point. If he's a flushing dog working too fast, no birds will be produced for the gun because the flushes will occur out of gun range. A grouse dog must be calm and easily managed. He should not require heavy handling. Voice commands should be kept to a minimum because these will cause grouse to depart in a hurry. The only sounds interrupting the coverts should be those of his bell (to indicate his location when it's heard and his point when it's silent) and occasional whistle signals. The grouse dog must work heavy cover thoroughly in search of grouse scent. When he does smell grouse, he must have enough confidence in himself to go on point immediately. Creeping in just won't do because the grouse will flush too soon. The hunter then goes forward for the flush, which could be fifty feet or more in front of the dog. Because grouse are extremely fast and hard to hit anyway, the hunter has an advantage now in that he knows a bird is present. The dog, pointing a good distance away, will allow the hunter to prepare himself physically and mentally for a fast, difficult shot.

A grouse dog must be willing to work rugged areas. A dog that avoids rough cover won't find grouse for you. By the same token, a brush-buster crashing the coverts at break-neck speed in his quest to get to the next ridge will also fail. A grouse dog hunts close. He's thorough and methodical in his field manner. If he's a pointing dog, his points are hard, fas and immediate when grouse are scented. The dog must wan to hunt carefully because grouse won't tolerate a rough, care less dog. He'll have to be a superb retriever, willing to mar each fall. When the bird is downed, he'll have to search heav cover in order to reclaim the prize. A grouse dog must be flawless retriever that understands that the task is not con plete until all shot birds are recovered, no matter how di ficult. A grouse dog is special. He's calm, thorough, and smart. He's willing to hunt carefully in order to produce game. He'll have to work hard all day if necessary and do this work with style and finesse. A good grouse dog is of necessity a truly finished gun dog that handles his quarry the only way it can be handled.

Grouse hunting is a sport best enjoyed with a polished gun dog. Picking the right dog is critical. Of course, it's usually best to start with a pup although you may opt for an older dog. If so, the type of handling the older dog received is crucially important. If he was handled sensibly with love and positive reinforcement--through patient, natural means--he could make a great grouse hunting companion once you and he become *friends.*

Many sportsmen have biases regarding grouse dogs. While some argue in favor of a particular gender or color, these considerations are largely insignificant. Others claim a grouse dog must be *close* while others want their dogs *out there* with head held high, catching grouse scent in the wind. If the dog is so close as to be under foot, he's probably too sluggish. Just because he's walking in the woods with you doesn't mean he's working. By the same token, the wider ranging dog, while probably working, can be self-hunting and no matter how good his nose is, you won't see his performance. Others like their dogs fast, but if he's too fast, he may overrun or bump the nervous grouse, never allowing the hunter to get a shot. But the slow dog, plodding along with the hunter, will find only those grouse which chance has placed in his path.

So how can you select the best possible grouse dog? For starters, only consider those dogs of good field breeding. You may as well rule out show dogs of non-field background since their characteristics usually do not lend themselves to excellence in the field. You should also rule out the *slugs*, those uninspiring dogs that totally lack style and animation. At the opposite extreme, don't even consider the hyper, ultra-high spirited, overly fast, big-running field-breds whose bird-finding desire and intensity overshadow their desire to hunt as a team member. Sure, they have the nose and drive, but you won't enjoy chasing them.

Photo 55 by: Bob Karacson.
This pup shows interest in the scents, sights, and sounds in her new environment. She is sensible and loves to point. Her parents are accomplished grouse dogs from a long line of class gun dogs. She's a good bet!

The purpose of grouse hunting is to hunt grouse, not dogs, and nothing spoils a grouse hunt surer than an out-of-control, out-of-range dog. A real big running dog is generally suited to open country, not the grouse woods.

So, where do you go for a grouse dog? Those who promote *foot hunting dogs* may have a very good line--but then again, they just may have sluggish, plodding *klutzes*. The firey field breds offer your best option, but be careful! If the dogs from the field line were, over the generations bred for performance, they'll have the nose, the desire, the style, the stamina, and the ability for which you're looking. But there must be something else, too. Your field-bred grouse dog must be calm, intelligent, and tractable. If his field-bred parents and grandparents had these qualities, and if the pup you're looking at seems to have a happy, laid back yet inquisitive attitude, he's probably a good one. Take him for a little romp in the field. If he likes handling, that's good. If he shows an interest in insects, movement, blowing leaves, or other things in his environment, that's great. If he does not show signs of timidity, cowardice, aggression, or flightiness, he'll probably suit your purposes nicely. Then, check his pedigree. If the dogs close-up in his background are obscure and of questionable ability, think twice. If the dog is of a line with inherent physical defects such as hip dysplasia, rule him out. Also, do not even consider him if his background is largely show-breeding in which field performance was not stressed. Then look at his parents. Are they birdy, calm, smart, stylish, companionable, and zealous in the field? If so, your pup is probably a good bet. Take him. The rest is up to you. Give him the training and the experience to make him something special--a grouse dog!

---

*Education is an on-going process.
Learning continues throughout
life--yours and your dog's.*

26

Training With Pigeons

In order to keep your bird dog *polished up* during the off
season or prepared for an up-coming bird season, don't
overlook the value of pigeons in training. These wonderful
birds, though not really game birds, have game-bird qualities.
They are easily controlled and can be used effectively use to
train your gun dog.

Pigeons are desirable for training for many reasons. First
of all, they behave like a game bird when used in a bird
launcher, restraint harness, or wing strap. If you use the
harness or wing strap, you can take the birds out into the field
and drop them off in such a way as to be able to work your dog
into their scent. The wing strap will permit the bird to move
around some, leaving plenty of scent. When you bring your
dog into the vicinity of these birds, begin to *Whoa* him as
necessary or, if a checkchord is used, step on or hold the cord
so he doesn't bust into your restrained bird. Once everything

Photo 56 by: Len Jenkins.
Ah! This looks and smells interesting! A young setter has her first contact with a live bird. A harnessed pigeon is extremely useful in dog training. Bird contact should begin at an early age.

is set and your dog is nicely on point, you can tease (or test) him a bit by maneuvering the bird, pulling on the wing strap string. When you are ready to have the bird flush, simply jerk the string sharply and as the release harness comes apart, the bird flies. At this point, you can either shoot the bird or let it fly, either away to its own loft or into the wild. If you shoot the bird, you can work on keeping your dog steady to wing and shot as well as retrieving. While working in this manner, you can control all variables, including dog, bird, scent, flush, and timing, providing your dog with plenty of action and simulating a successful hunt. A young dog, in this stage, should be on a checkcord until he is steady to wing and shot and points hard.

For a little more sophistication and excitement, you can also use a mechanical or electronic launcher. These devices throw the bird into the air and forces it to fly strongly. While the launcher is very effective, it is considerably more expensive than the bird release harness. The use of the launcher can simulate a game bird rise although the bird will not be able to move around much prior to launching. Therefore, you won't get the benefit of much scent as you would with the simple, inexpensive and highly effective harness.

One of the good things about pigeons is that they are easily managed. If you raise your own pigeons, they can be trained to return to their loft if you choose not to shoot them. If you don't want to bother maintaining these birds, you can purchase them very inexpensively at livestock auctions or simply trap them in barns. If you wish, you can also buy them from breeders although the price would understandably be higher than at an auction. Prior to use, the pigeons can be maintained by simply providing them with clean shelter in a small pen plus grain (cracked corn is fine), grit, and plenty of clean water in a deep container (not a shallow poultry fount).

If you decide to raise your own pigeons, you can buy a few pairs and train them to remain in their new home by keeping them confined for two to three weeks before letting them out. They will usually return to their new home and the shelter, food, and water provided there. A bob-type door, readily available through dog supply houses or feed mills, is easily installed, and pigeons quickly learn how to return to their home. Of course, you don't need the bob-type door if you leave a small door open or provide an opening for their exit and return although predators can also freely enter as well as the pigeons.

Pigeons reproduce quickly, and before long your population will increase. The young birds will know their home and do not need to be trained to return like their parents. They will provide a renewable training resource for keeping your dog's skills well-honed. At this point you can really get a lot done with your dog because you can shoot the birds, allowing

Photo 57 by: Terry Krueger.
Pigeons trained to return to their loft can be used repeatedly in training. After being snapped free from the pigeon harness or sprung from the mechnical launcher, they simply fly back "home". The use of pigeons will greatly simplify the training process.

your dog to work on all skills such as winding the birds, pointing staunchly, and retrieving the downed *game* to hand.

While pigeons are useful for training your dog, they provide a relaxing and fascinating hobby themselves; you may find that you actually derive much pleasure from maintaining your training flock. The pigeons have a very interesting society involving division of labor, territoriality, and family structure. The birds are monogamous, and both males and females share the tasks of incubation and care of the young. While the birds are very good flyers, they are also calm and tame. They are nothing like pheasants or quail which are quite often nervous around human beings. If you buy rollers, an interesting smaller pigeon breed, get set for fascinating air shows as your birds soar, glide, plummet and do acrobatic tricks and flips in mid-air. Although calm and easily caught when needed, the pigeons used in training will fly strongly for your dog. This is drastically different from recently liberated pen-reared quail and pheasants which usually just run or sit, making a training experience *fizzle*. For use in training, a pigeon is more of a game bird than most pen-reared quail or pheasants, hands down.

Training with pigeons is fun because the experience is so comprehensive. You can simulate all aspects of a real hunt in your training because the pigeons cooperate. Your dog will come to associate training with actually connecting on a bird, and you have the advantage of being in control of every aspect. Once you have brushed up your experienced dog's skills or developed those of a young one, you are ready for real action. Your dog has the techniques down pat. You have the control needed because your dog associates hunting with you with the actual finding and shooting of game. Your dog has learned to put it all together, thanks to pigeons. Now you and he are ready for the uplands in quest of your favorite game bird.

> *You can't train your own bird dog without using actual birds in the training process.*

27

The Field Dog Stud Book

The Field Dog Stud Book (FDSB) is the registry for purebred dogs of any of the sporting breeds. The vast majority of dogs registered with FDSB are pointers and English setters although field-bred dogs of a variety of other pointing, flushing, and retrieving breeds are also registered.

The FDSB has not lost its focus. A dog registered with this registry is typically a working dog which embodies the traits hunters find desirable. These dogs typically possess great stamina and durability. They have inordinately developed noses for finding game and an unquenchable thirst for sport. These are useful dogs indeed.

The FDSB does not prescribe particular conformation standards, but it is a registry accepting dogs of the highest superiority regarding the standards that count. Since most FDSB registered dogs are working dogs, those which are unfit for hard work in the field are naturally culled because they can't cut it on the job. As a result, those individuals lacking nose, desire, heart, hunting instinct, biddability, stability of personality, intelligence, physical soundness, and stamina are not kept as hunting dogs and typically are not bred to meet an artificial conformation standard. It would be frivolous for a sportsman to pride himself in owning a clumsy, neurotic, unintelligent animal which can't hunt because the hunt's been bred out of him in deference to meeting a conformation standard. Consequently, it would be unlikely that such a dog or its progeny would find their way into the FDSB registry. Because the emphasis has been on performance, the FDSB can be credited with saving the English setter and pointer as gun dogs. The same salvation is available to superior strains of other fine breeds as well as evidenced by the weekly publication of registrations in the <u>American Field</u> for a variety of sporting breeds.

Besides maintaining the registry, the FDSB provides a host of other services and functions. It provides for enrollment of litters produced from a registered sire and dam. Much useful information is available from the registry regarding field dogs and their history and development in North America. The FDSB sanctions many field trials of the highest caliber which provide the acid test for some of the most competitive and accomplished dogs in the entire sporting world. The <u>American Field</u> is a weekly publication which provides much vital information. The <u>Field</u>, first established in 1874, is considered the recognized authority for field-bred dogs. It is available by subscription from the American Field Publishing Company, 542 South Dearborn, Chicago, Illinois 60605-1528.

While the FDSB registered dog is usually a fine-looking animal in its own right, don't expect it to look exactly like dogs you might see in the show ring. A different standard is expected of the gun dog. If the chest is large enough to accommodate the heart and if the cranium is large enough to accommodate a remarkable intelligence, the dog adequately meets the *standard*. Likewise, if the skeletal structure, eyes, neurological system, coat, legs, etc. allow the dog to go all day, working hard and producing in high style, the dog has fully met the standard. Such a dog is indeed a fine representative of his breed and man does not need to engineer artificial standards at the expense of the essential traits. To arbitrarily decide, for instance, that droopy eyes which catch pollen and debris, or a large skeletal structure prone to dysplasia is desired in a dog's conformation would lead to the deterioration of a breed for the field. The FDSB was wise to leave well-enough alone in this area. What's in his head and in his heart is what makes the dog.

The FDSB accepts dogs from other registries provided proper procedures are followed and full documentation is provided for their registration. By the same token, there is a procedure by which FDSB-registered dogs can be registered in other registries such as the American Kennel Club (AKC). Some sportspeople enjoy dual registration because it allows for competition in field trials of other registries. If this is what you're interested in, go ahead and dual register. It's good for both your dog as well as the other registry. A high quality, hunting-style FDSB dog could improve the field qualities of dogs in other registries while providing healthy competition. It is vital that the hunting qualities of fine sporting breeds not be lost. If you see no prospect for competition, however, dual registration would serve no purpose. But if you choose to compete, you'll enjoy it. You also should do everything possible to support the field tests of other registries. Let those of influence know that you encourage tests of field performance in order to preserve the hunting qualities of fine dogs. Be supportive at all times!

All high-quality gun dogs should be registered with FDSB. Many people have made a wholehearted commitment to the development and preservation of fine shooting dogs. If records weren't kept through registration, we would not have consistently fine gun dogs available today. When you buy a pup from FDSB-registered stock, register him. If you breed fine registered dogs, enroll the litters and encourage individual registration of the progeny. In this manner, you are doing your part to advance quality gun dogs while continuing the FDSB's fine tradition. Besides that, a registered dog is a dog of higher value than one that is not registered. Though papers don't hunt, dogs developed from field stock do. You owe it to yourself, as well as the breed of your choice, to register.

> *Control your dog; don't let him control you.*

28

The American Kennel Club

While most English setters and pointers are registered with the FDSB, the majority of Gordon and Irish setters, retrievers, spaniels, and versatile dogs are registered with the American Kennel Club (AKC), a registry and corporation committed to the advancement of purebred dogs. According to Section 2 of a charter granted the AKC by the State of New York by Special Act of its Legislature, the objectives of the AKC are varied yet consistent with its purpose to advance purebred dogs. The objectives of the AKC are many-fold and consistent with ensuring the improvement and purity of pedigreed dogs. These objectives include:

- The enforcement and adoption of rules governing shows and field trials,
- The regulation of conduct by persons involved with purebred dogs, including breeding, exhibiting, registering, purchasing or selling,

Photo 58 by: Randy Mapus.

This classy field-type setter is dual registered with FDSB and AKC as Prairie Buckboard and Prairie Phantom Buckboard JH, respectively. "Bucky," owned by Randy Mapus of Castalia, Ohio, has done extremely well in AKC field trial placements.

- The prevention and punishment of fraud in connection with registration,

- The publication of an official stud book and kennel gazette, and

- The maintenance of activities and policies necessary to advance the study, appreciation, propagation, showing and registering of purebred dogs.

The major competitive functions held by the AKC are dog shows and field trials. Owners and breeders can exhibit their dogs at these functions to demonstrate their dog's conformational quality relative to the breed standard or field ability in accordance with rules and regulations established for spaniels, retrievers, and pointing dogs. Copies of the respec tive rules and regulations can be procured free of charge by writing The American Kennel Club, Inc., 51 Madison Avenue, New York, NY 10010.

While some breeders stress bench standards and others stress field performance in their breeding programs, there are some who strive to produce a dual purpose dog. As a sportsman, you should look to a kennel which breeds field dogs. There is no point in trying to turn a show dog into an athletic field performer if the show dog lacks the inclination to hunt. There are entire families of dogs which have lost the desire or ability to hunt because hunting ability was not a criterion on which breeding stock was selected. It appears that some strains of sporting dogs are becoming less adept at hunting. Such dogs might be following the course of other breeds which have deviated from the working qualities that originally distinguished them from other breeds. Don't com-

Photo 59 by: Christine Tabone.
You might really enjoy field trials whether they are sponsored byAKC, American Field, National Shoot to Retrieve Field Trial Association, or various breed clubs.

plicate your gun dog training by selecting a dog that lacks ability, no matter how close he approaches the ideal conformation standard. If the dog can work energetically and skillfully in the field all day, his conformation is just fine. Go to a breeder who has not lost sight of what a sporting dog should be. There are kennels that specialize in performance dogs in all the fine sporting breeds registered with AKC.

The field trials can provide you with a source of much pleasure and satisfaction. If you develop a class gun dog, why not enter him in one of the AKC trials? You might enjoy this even more than hunting! Your AKC registered dog can also be entered in National Shoot to Retrieve trials and American Field trials provided he's dual registered with FDSB. There are many possibilities!

All interaction with your dog is training.

29

Today's English Setter

The modern American-bred English setter is one of the world's great gun dog breeds. While the breed itself had its origin in England, individual dogs were brought to North America and became the nucleus of fine American breeding programs which required first-class handling of American game birds under American conditions. Many fine dogs emanated from these early setters, including Gladstone, Count Gladstone, Phil Essig, Sports Peerless, Feagin's Mohawk Pal, Mississippi Zev and others. Many modern setters trace their origins to these excellent gun dogs.

While setters were evolving in North America, there was still considerable breed development in England. It is this breeding that is most responsible for the differences between the field type-setter and the show-type today.

The breed has had a long and enigmatic history of over four hundred years. In the very early days, the prime concern

Photo 60 by Terry Krueger.

Charlen's Smokey on point! Today's English setter is a stylist supreme.

with developing *setting* dogs was to have the dog crouch very low to the ground when game was found, thereby allowing the hunter to cast a net over the birds. These *setting* dogs represented a combination of blood lines from a variety of breeds such as spaniels and Spanish pointers. Dogs which maintained a prolonged point were valued most, and those individuals with the most highly developed pointing tendency were bred to others of similar inclination, even if breeds were mixed. The pointing tendency was the trait for which early breeders (hunters) selected their foundation stock. These early *setting* dogs were largely land spaniel in their genetic makeup although they were the precursors of what was to become the English setter.

Edward Laverack is generally credited with being most responsible for resolving the land spaniel type English *setting* dogs into the breed we know as English setters today. Some of Laverack's inbreeding and outcrossing methods may have been criticized and even held suspect, but he nonetheless created a type of dog which we now consider the English setter. There were others in England also breeding setters, and it was during this period in the early to mid-1800's that many of the English dogs found their way to North America.

R. L. Purcell Llewellin, a Welshman, was very instrumental in developing a strain of setters by mixing the Laverack strain with others of similar quality. There is some mystery, however, as to what lines were bred because it appears, secrets were kept. It is generally suspected that Gordon, Russian, and Irish setters, as well as pointers and spaniels, were incorporated into the foundation of this early stock. In any event, it was Llewellin who developed the fine strain of field dogs which became known as Llewellin setters. While some controversy raged in England regarding the breed's development into rather diverse strains, the American English setters were also developing. Throughout this period, imports were made and many of these imports were bred with the native stock. The Llewellins soon achieved fame as trial dogs and gained easier acceptance into early American field breeding than did their Laverack counterparts. Consequently, the Laverack type evolved basically into the show setter while the Llewellin, either kept pure as a strain in order to preserve the Llewellin name or blended with native setter lines, became the field-type.

Today, most gun dog enthusiasts who own an English setter own the field-type, the one most similar to the original Llewellin. This is a superior gun dog in many respects. English setters have a tremendous desire to please and accept the hunter's restrictions easily in order to work properly. Etiquette is important to the full enjoyment of the hunt. The English setter obligingly channels his energy and desire to work the game willingly in accordance with his owner's rules. He finds game, points it, marks its fall, and retrieves it to hand in a controlled and civilized manner. He willingly modifies his stalking nature to make stylish points a pretty fair distance from the quarry so as not to spook it into flight before the hunter could be in position to make the shot. The dog will bound out after a fallen bird and recover it in a fine retrieve, relinquishing the bird to hand before going out again to continue the quest. All the while the dog works, he does it with animation and style. He gives his all to his work and derives pleasure from both the pursuit of game and the pleasure he brings his owner. Today's English setter is indeed a class individual in the field.

Besides being a superb gun dog, the setter is an exceptional companion dog who thrives on maintaining close association with his owner and the family to which he belongs. Setters love children, and they love to please in general.

They're an intelligent dog with a highly developed sensitivity. They obediently and enthusiastically work for their owner's satisfaction. These dogs dispel the old myth that a gun dog is never a pet. On the contrary, the closer the association with their owner, the better the field performance.

The modern field setter is a beautiful animal that moves in a graceful, animated fashion. While typically smaller than the show-style dog, they have a different appearance and represent a functional beauty lacking in their show-ring distant cousins. They move in a fluid manner and deliver an electrifying, spectacular show when working.

The English setter is particularly adept at working thick coverts in the northern, colder parts of the United States. This is where they seemed to achieve prominence early in their development on this side of the Atlantic. The heavier coat, more pronounced retrieving instinct, and close working tendencies have endeared them to grouse and woodcock hunters of New England, Appalachia, and the Midwest. Since their early days up north, however, they have also become accomplished at working other kinds of game in the South and West. While many setters are still naturally close-working dogs, certain strains have also been developed which are naturally bigger running, much like the pointer. Whether you're interested in a big-running or close-working setter, there are individuals within this breed to meet your specific needs.

Setters are exceptionally good at working all game birds if given adequate experience. A finished grouse dog will adjust to hunting pheasants or quail. There is no upland game bird a setter won't hunt.

The field sport enthusiast who has never owned a setter is missing the pleasure of working with this very fine breed. Because some setters are quite sensitive, they must be handled carefully to bring out all their virtues. Such dogs simply would not do well for someone who is indifferent to his dog or harsh in his handling. But for the hunter who wants an easy handling, classy, beautiful, dynamic field dog who will work hard and long to enhance the hunt with bird finds and high style, today's English setter is hard to beat.

By never allowing your dog unrestrained freedom, he will learn he needs you for success. You are always the main component of the hunting experience.

30

The Environmental Factor: Top Performance More Than Luck

N̲o sportsman can expect to be in the best of health and physically capable of strenuous sport if his body is constantly wracked by environmental stress. If a place of human habitation does not provide the environment required for decent, healthful living, the occupants suffer and a public agency might condemn the structure as *unfit for human habitation*. Yet many sportsmen, while concerned for their personal environmental quality, do not pay close attention to the environmental quality of their dog's place of habitation. These same sportsmen, however, expect optimal performance from their dogs in the field.

Edward J. Polk

What environmental conditions should be met to keep your dog healthy, strong and happy? Though no public agency will condemn your kennel as *unfit for canine habitation*, some self-evaluation might be in order to help your dog work to his fullest potential for you. The following environmental considerations will help achieve this:

Water

- Is your dog supplied with fresh water daily? This water should be safe for his consumption. The dish itself should be free of algae growth, mud, and debris.

Food

- Is your dog fed a ration sufficiently high in protein and suitable for his *life style*? If this food is moldy or contaminated, it should be discarded.

Shelter

- Does your dog's house provide him protection from environmental forces such as wind, snow, rain and heat? Bedding should be clean and changed from time to time.

Exercise Area

- Is your dog's run clean and free of excessive amounts of excrement? Runs should be raked, shoveled, rinsed, or otherwise cleaned daily. A good chlorine disinfectant should be used periodically.

Safety

- Is your dog's kenneling area free of potential hazards such as projecting nails or wire as well as debris which could cause physical injury in some way? If so, all safety hazards should be eliminated to protect your dog's health and save you a potentially heavy veterinary expense.

Sunlight/Shade

- Does sunlight penetrate to your dog's living quarters? While sunlight is a good natural disinfectant as well as a source of pleasure for your dog, he should also have access to some shade in case the sun and heat become too intense.

Drainage

- Are your grounds free of stagnant, standing water which supports mosquitoes, flies, and bacteria? Good drainage is particularly important in areas plagued by heartworm since it limits mosquito breeding places.

Internal and External Parasites

- Are you careful to rid your dog of worms, fleas, and ticks? No dog should play host to parasites because of owner neglect. Maintaining high environmental standards will do much to minimize the adverse effects of parasites.

Vectors

- Are you inadvertently providing harborage for undesirable animals which could be carriers of disease? For instance, sloppy dog food handling and feeding practices could result in rat and mouse infestation of your kennel facilities. Also, poor disposal of dog excrement and soiled food could result in excessive harborage of flies. The careful use of rodenticides and insecticides might be necessary, although your first defense against infestation is sanitation.

Communicable diseases

- Is your dog properly immunized against distemper, parainfluenza, parvo virus, hepatitis, leptospirosis and rabies? There is no excuse for your dog having these diseases since effective immunizations are available and should be administered on a regular schedule.

Your dog is a good friend who asks for little while working hard for you. Since he will give you his best effort in the uplands, doesn't it make sense for you to ensure that he can work up to his full potential? This potential cannot be reached if his system is plagued by environmental stress you can control. A little preventive environmental maintenance will result in maximum sport and pleasure afield. Both you and your dog deserve each other's best!

A little preventive environmental maintenance will result in maximum sport and pleasure afield

---

31

Home Quail Covey

If you enjoy wild game birds for their aesthetic value as well as their use as a valuable dog training resource, consider establishing a *wild* quail covey around your home. While you can't expect much success with quail if your home is not reasonably located within the Bobwhite's natural range, this wonderful little bird will adapt to your nurturing and behave like a wild bird if you give it a chance. The excitement of a covey rise rivals grouse hunting in its own right. But when you consider the value you can get from quail for fine tuning your grouse dog with wild bird contact on both coveys and singles, your efforts are more than rewarded.

In establishing a covey around your home, you must procure some birds. There are many quail farms around the country, many of which are advertised in sporting publications. Because game bird farms are usually state licensed and approved, you can also contact your state's Department of

Natural Resources for locally available birds. If you start with quail chicks, there is considerable work in rearing them. They must be maintained under the proper temperature. Your pen must have sufficient space to accommodate the chicks and be designed so as to prevent the birds from piling up and suffocating. A game bird ration and constant supply of clean, fresh drinking water in a poultry fount must always be available. You could check with the game bird farm regarding techniques for raising quail. If you wish to take a shortcut, you can begin with started birds and get your covey started sooner. Regardless of the age you begin with, make sure you follow your state's regulation for the possession of game birds.

Your birds should be transferred into a screened flight pen in the vicinity in which you wish to establish your covey. Make sure the birds are in a place where they are not constantly harassed by dogs, cats, or people since you don't want them to become accustomed to these things to the point that they are easy prey for predators. After the birds have been established in their new location for a while, release a few of them. They will enjoy their freedom but will remain near the area of the flight pen. In fact, if the pen sets off the ground on legs, the liberated birds will probably covey up at night under the pen because they want to be close to the ones still in captivity. It is these captive birds which will hold your covey in the location of the release.

The area in which you release the birds must have sufficient cover to protect the birds from the elements as well as predators. It should contain some natural foods such as weed seeds, wild grapes, and berries. The quail will soon learn to forage for food, but in order to hold them in the area, you're going to have to augment the natural supply of food by providing cracked corn or other feeds. This should be scattered near the flight pen, but you're also going to have to set out a feede in a suitable location and keep it filled, especially in winter. When you initially release your first birds, be sure to also provide grit and fresh water. Before long, the birds will learn to find water on their own, and the environment will provide plenty of natural grit.

Periodically you should release a few more birds from the captives. These will then join their liberated compatriots in the *wild covey*. Don't, however, release all the birds. The captives will still hold the liberated ones for you. The next spring, if you wish, you could release the remaining birds to the wild, and hopefully they will replenish your *wild covey* after natural winter losses and reproduce. It seems that the liberated birds soon teach the newly liberated ones how to survive on their own.

Once your birds are established and have become strong flyers, you will derive a lot of pleasure from them. Their calls are delightful and the presence of quail adds a new dimension to enjoying your home environment. But besides their wonderful aesthetic value, these fine feathered little bomb shells can really help you with training and developing your gun dog. Granted, your quail will not become woodland wildlife, but they will occupy brushy areas and *edge*. They're great for working a young dog because they'll sit pretty tight. They impart considerable scent, and what's really nice is that once you get the covey up, you can mark the singles and go after them. Even though you're not shooting the birds over your dog, you can work on everything else--winding, pointing, whistle signals, quartering, and style. These birds are far better than pheasants for training because they won't run much. You can get a lot of mileage from each covey because of the singles after the initial rise. These birds also smell and act wild, with no human scent on them. The greatest advantage to maintaining quail, however, is that their presence is predictable in your field since you've been nurturing them and holding them in by providing food, shelter, and cover. You can now take your young dog afield in the off-season for training and practice, knowing full well there will be some action, compliments of your home quail covey.

Make sure you follow your state's regulations for the possession of game birds.

32

The Quarry

While there are many different game birds you can hunt with your upland gun dog, this chapter is necessarily limited to the most frequently hunted species. This is not intended to be a treatise on game birds. There are several birds which provide fine sport which are not mentioned here primarily because of their limited range or popularity with gunners. Nonetheless, a quality gun dog will be capable of hunting all game birds although it takes time and experience for him to become adept at all types of bird-handling techniques. A top-notch pheasant dog, for instance, may only possess minimal or passable skill at handling grouse or woodcock. With experience, such a dog can become better at handling these woodland birds although some dogs are simply better at certain kinds of hunting than others. While many classy big-running quail dogs can adjust to working close on grouse, some find it contrary to their nature. You should expect your dog to handle a variety of game, but you must also allow for the dog's natural inclinations. All dogs can be improved, and all dogs can hunt a variety of game. To expect every dog, however, to hunt all game with equal finish is a little unreasonable, particularly if the dog wasn't given much opportunity to learn the habits of each bird. The birds mentioned here are typically hunted by today's pointing, flushing, versatile, and retrieving breeds.

Ruffed Grouse

This regal game bird continues to be the obsession of many throughout New England, the upper Midwest, Eastern Canada, the Middle Atlantic states, Appalachia, and various scattered locations elsewhere in North America. Because of their excellent sporting qualities, some states are even intro-

Photo 61 by: Paul Carson, Ruffed Grouse Society.
This spectacular display of grouse gallantry was captured on camera by the Ruffed Grouse Society Editor, Paul Carson.

Photo 62 by: Paul Carson, Ruffed Grouse Society.
The ruffed grouse abounds in the thickets of the Tittabawassee and other forested areas of North America. Locating grouse is best done with a pointing dog.

ducing grouse into areas where they're not native if the habitat for the grouse planting is suitable. This is a fast, explosive bird that has thrilled many gunners with its challenging speed. Grouse, frequently called *pats* here in Michigan, provide bird hunting opportunities in brushy and wooded areas. These birds can be easily handled by a dog, provided he doesn't get too close. If he does, the bird will take flight, usually only to be heard, not seen. If your dog crowds pheasants or quail too much, he'll have problems with grouse. While grouse often sit tight, they flush wildly at other times and often run. A top-notch grouse dog should handle them at a pretty good distance and anticipate their nervous and sometimes erratic behavior.

Grouse are indeed challenging birds. Successful hunters work in areas containing both adequate cover and food to meet the birds' needs. The grouse are usually not real numerous, but it doesn't take many to make the gunner want to carry on his obsession with hunting the king of game birds.

Woodcock

While the grouse is the king of game birds, the chunky little woodcock must be the court jester. It's amazing that he can get his round plump body and ungainly long bill airborne. Who could believe that such a comical-looking little bird could provide sporting shots and endear himself to grouse hunters who often hunt woodcock as an incidental part of a grouse hunt!

Woodcock provide fast action. When the birds are migrating, you and your dog will most likely find many birds. They will be found in moist areas where cover is thick, frequently in alder thickets. Although the birds are not very large, they look much bigger than they really are when flying. They may not appear to be fast, but they're nonetheless often hard to hit due to their erratic, dipping flight. While most hunters don't seem to go out specifically for woodcock, they probably revere the silly-looking little timberdoodle in their hearts. Woodcock are a superb game bird in their own right and have provided much action for grouse hunters. They've saved many hunts by holding nicely for dogs on point, allowing the gunner to have some quality hunting when grouse were scarce or uncooperative. While some dogs are said to refuse to retrieve woodcock, most will hunt them with high style and retrieve them satisfactorily.

If the woodcock were truly appreciated as a game bird, more hunters would be hunting them as their primary quarry and treating grouse as a secondary bird. After hunting woodcock with your gun dog, you just might find yourself saying you're going grouse hunting, but in your heart you'll know it's woodcock you're after!

Photo 63 by: Paul Carson, Ruffed Grouse Society.
Woodcock enjoy moist coverts where they can forage for worms. During their migrations, they provide fast shooting and great sport.

Bobwhite Quail

Gentleman Bob is the gentleman's game bird. He'll obligingly provide great classic sport and treat your dog to an opportunity to hunt a bird that cooperates elegantly.

Quail are most common in the American South and much of the Midwest. They are the primary game bird hunted in Dixie and have provided high quality sport for generations. These wonderful birds will sit tight for a dog and explode wildly when flushed. They tend to covey up during hunting season and provide much excitement as the covey rises in unison. The wise gunner will select one or two specific birds as the covey takes flight. He'll then be able to pursue the singles as the broken covey settles down again. After collecting birds shot on the initial covey rise, the singles provide first class shooting. They should be marked as they land and hunted one at a time. The dog work will be superb. Once you hunt these fine little bombshells, you'll want to do it again.

Ringneck Pheasant

The bawdy, raucous pheasant is far from being a gentleman like the quail. This bird is unscrupulous in his field behavior. He'll do anything he wants to do to elude, out-run, out-sit, or out-smart you and your dog. He might take flight right under your nose or a mile down a hedge row. He might run clear across a stubble field or hide in a depression as you

Photo 64 by: George Dusseau.
Charlen's Smokey and Louise pause with the writer, Mike Jenkins, and Bill Bolyard during a recent Pelee Island, Ontario, Canada pheasant hunt.

and your dog simply pass him. The pheasant may hold tight for a nice point and then skulk away on your dog, leaving him there to look like a false pointer or a fool. The wily ringneck's his own bird. He'll play hard ball with you so get set to expect the unexpected. If you've been orthodox in your training strategy, you'll probably want to reassess the way you expect your dog to work if pheasants are the game you primarily hunt. In fact, if you're a pheasant hunter who is committed to hunting this bird, you should make sure your dog gets as much experience as possible hunting the real thing, the ringneck in the wild, rather than his more docile kin, planted game farm birds.

Pheasants are notorious for sitting tight and then skulking away or running off. Pointing dogs let you know when this happens because they'll go on point, then stalk, reestablish point, stalk, point, stalk, point, stalk... This certainly breaks the rules. Well, think about the nature of your quarry. He'll do anything to evade or outwit. If you're hunting pheasant exclusively, perhaps you'll just have to accept this point/stalk pattern when the birds won't hold. With enough practice on the cagey birds, however, your pointing dog will start to figure them out even though pheasant behavior can manifest itself in many unpredictable ways. A good pointing dog, given enough experience, will learn to handle the running bird by arcing around and ahead of the racing ringneck, heading him off, beating him at his own game. This takes time, but once your dog figures this out, he's on the road to being a pheasant dog.

The flushing and retrieving breeds are great for pheasants because they'll pursue the birds and drive them into flight if they insist on running, thus affording a shot. Pheasant hunting with a dog is exciting because of the gaudy ringneck's tough manner and hard-flying, hard-running habits. Once your dog and you realize that the bird is a master at deceit and evasion, you'll be on your way to enjoying one of the finest upland sports--pheasant hunting. Have you thought about a trip to South Dakota or Iowa lately?

Chukars

Hunting chukars in the rugged, semi-arid country they've adapted to in the American West is tough sport. The hunting conditions are rough and dry. The mountainous, barren terrain is hard on a dog's feet and poses unaccustomed difficulties. Because of lack of scent due to the dryness and the nature of the birds' not usually sitting tight for a close-working dog, you and your dog will have to cover a lot of country, working hard every inch of the way. Chukars are tough so you and your dog will have to toughen up accordingly and adapt to hunting in rough country when in search of these hard-flying dwellers of the rimrock and canyons.

Chukars can be hunted in other areas of North America as released shooting preserve birds. They afford good sport because they fly hard and far. Since they require mountainous dry country to meet their needs, you will not find wild chukars in the lush, green parts of North America. Hunting them on preserves, however, is a treat you may wish to experience.

Hungarian Partridge

The Hungarian partridge is a fine game bird in the fairly limited agricultural areas of Canada and the United States where it has been established. In fact, the prospect of its becoming a more important game bird increases all the time as various game departments are making new plants in grassland and farm country.

The Hun is similar to the bobwhite quail in that it will usually hold nicely for a pointing dog. These birds covey up like quail and rise in unison for a dramatic covey rise. The major difference, however, is that the Hungarian will fly a much greater distance before coming down. Because of this, a wider ranging dog, such as a pointer or setter, is preferred.

Watch for Hungarian partridge to become an integral part of the shooting scene in many areas. Like the reintroduction of wild turkeys, introduction of pheasant, grouse, and chukars to areas where they were never native, or the Michigan experience with the Szechwan pheasant, the Hungarian partridge just might become another wildlife success story providing much sport for gun dog enthusiasts.

Doves

Doves have an identity problem. Here in Michigan, like a few other states, doves are *song birds*, gracing the lawns of suburbia and gliding gracefully over grain fields in vast numbers. The same bird, however, is suddenly transformed into a hard-flying speedster of game-bird stature once it crosses the state line into Indiana.

Those in the Hoosier state are fortunate that they're able to utilize the abundant and prolific mourning dove as a game bird affording much quality shooting. When the doves are feeding in harvested grain fields, pointing dogs can be distracted into the fairly non-productive diversion of watching and foolishly pointing and chasing doves when they should be hunting quail or pheasants instead. Such a dog can, of course, be called from this activity and set back on track. However, this is a pretty good indication that dogs must be attracted to doves, apparently because they have natural game-bird qualities. While the upland gunner in search of quail or pheasant hunting will by-pass doves should his dog decide to work them, other gunners with dogs can avail themselves to the fast sport offered by the mourning dove.

Those hunters who station themselves in a blind at a field's edge where doves traverse from point to point while feeding can experience excellent shooting. After bringing down the hard-flying doves, they can send out a retrieving dog or flushing spaniel which has been sitting patiently in a blind with the hunter. The dog will relish the opportunity to utilize his retrieving talents, gaining much practice and pleasure marking the fallen birds and retrieving to hand. Ah! This is pleasant sport!

Waterfowl(and more!)

While this book is focused on developing a gun dog suitable for upland game, there is a possibility that the upland shooter will take an occasional duck while hunting in marshy, boggy areas or set up a blind in a harvested corn field to hunt Canada geese. Perhaps the gunner does not wish to take up

Edward J. Polk

Photo 65 by: Gordon Lewis.

A raft of waterfowl at Plum Island, Massachusetts.

the sport of waterfowl hunting over open water but prefers to simply use his upland shooting dog to take occasional ducks and geese. Perhaps he's the kind of gunner who espouses the Continental attitude that a gun dog should be *versatile*.

Hunting geese from an above ground or pit blind in a corn field requires quite a bit of effort and commitment. The hunter must construct the blind, set out decoys, and call in the geese. The dog of choice in this type of situation would be one of the retriever or versatile breeds which is content to sit patiently with the gunner and wait. The dog is then sent out to retrieve the downed bird after marking its fall or upon direction by the hunter. A quality retriever could make this activity rewarding and pleasurable, affording a whole new opportunity for diversified hunting. A dog like this could be used to retrieve geese in a corn field one day and hunt grouse or pheasants the next.

Provided the gunner has a duck stamp and follows legal practices, he can shoot an occasional duck while hunting near swamps and bogs while in search of traditional upland game birds such as woodcock or pheasant. Although doing this might be the forte of a versatile breed enthusiast or of a traditional duck hunter who only hunts upland game as a secondary interest, waterfowl might be of interest to others if it's abundant and if the hunter is inclined to take an occasional duck. A good retriever, versatile dog, or spaniel will usually find the downed duck without any problem. In fact, almost any dog of any sporting breed which has been trained to retrieve on command will search out downed game and retrieve a duck. Even though they're upland dogs, most of these breeds don't shy away from water and consequently will search for a bird in swampy areas. Of course, you would not be dropping a bird over open water. It would be very unfair to expect an upland gun dog who has never had any experience retrieving birds shot over open water to search out and find a duck dropped there. If you want to shoot ducks over open water, you should take up the fine sport of waterfowl hunting and do it right by training your dog to enter the water on command to retrieve downed waterfowl in a manner befitting a fine duck dog. Like upland shooting, waterfowl shooting has its own appeal and requires its own specialized discipline to do it properly. However, should you shoot an occasional duck flying in an area where it would drop on land, not open water, you should expect your upland dog to make the retrieve. Sportsmen and women do all in their power to make sure downed game is always retrieved, never wasted. Ours is a sport for gentlemen and ladies who carry on the sporting tradition in accordance with an ethic which values wildlife.

While a purist would probably shun shooting ducks with an upland dog, the spaniel or versatile devotee may not. In fact, there's a good chance such a hunter may even wish to hunt rabbits with his versatile dog or spaniel! Of course, the traditional upland bird hunter would probably also be a traditional rabbit hunter if he hunted rabbits at all. He would probably opt for a traditional rabbit dog, a baying merry beagle that hunts rabbits *right*. There is a place for tradition, isn't there? But of course, beagles don't retrieve. Oh, well, there's a special breed for everyone. But is there any reason why dedicated sportsmen can't own more than one kind of dog, each specializing in the various game they prefer hunting?

> *You should expect your dog to handle a variety of game, but you must also allow for the dog's natural inclinations.*

33

Save Our Sport

The sport of hunting is in jeopardy. Network news programs, the Humane Society, animal rights activists, preservationists, environmental groups, local special interest groups, and individuals question the value of hunting and seek further restrictions. This is a widespread trend, and it seems that none of the most vocal critics of our sport make mention of the good we have done through game area land acquisition, habitat development, law enforcement, and scientific research, all primarily funded by hunters' money from sales of licenses, stamps, special permits, and firearms and ammunition taxes. The trend is national in scope, and the war of words is intensifying. If something isn't done, it is possible hunting will be banned even on private property as well as wildlife areas hunters have purchased by paying license and permit fees.

Our numbers are declining annually. The politicians are being influenced more and more by the non-hunting majority. Hunters are plagued with a bad reputation generally. The

Photo 66 by: Valrie Lewis.

Moonglow's Magic Cloud is on point with owner, Gordon Lewis, going in to flush a New Hampshire ringneck! Hunting is best enjoyed behind a finished gun dog that does it all and does it in style!

national concern for banning hand guns and our preoccupation with violence in our major cities is getting mixed up with hunters and the constitutionally guaranteed right to bear arms. It is time we recognize that hunters are under fire and assertively do something about reversing this trend before it is too late.

The first thing we must do is clean up our image. Hunters should pride themselves on continuing a time-honored sport. It is a sport in which rules must be followed and for which we *pay to play*. No one has subsidized our sport but ourselves. Yet the public often perceives us as cold-blooded, crazed killers of animals. The image of the unsportsman-like hunter still prevails because there are unsportsman-like individuals among us who perpetrate the tarnished image. It's time we all do something about it through further resolve. The game laws are to be obeyed. Littering is a lingering physical reminder of lack of respect for the land. Damage to signs, wires, and private property by gunfire is evidence of an irresponsible person's being allowed to carry a dangerous weapon. The unnecessary killing of non-game animals or excessive legal killing of legal game has no place in our ethic. We all must do something about the unsportsman-like hunters by letting them know that their actions are wrong and that if there's not a change, our sport may someday be a thing of the past. If they won't change, don't condone their gross conduct by going hunting with them. Perhaps if education and a few words won't help, ostracism will.

Let the public know that you value wildlife. A good place to start is by making sure you don't take shots which will result in only wounding out-of-range wildlife. When game is shot, insist on recovery of all downed birds. Let our critics know that we pride ourselves on recovery of wounded wildlife by training our dogs to search out and retrieve the game we've brought down. Hunting with a well-trained dog which retrieves will communicate our concern for wildlife and will foster the notion that our sport is one for ladies and gentlemen.

Over the last few years the number of hunters has dropped significantly. With this decline in numbers is a necessary decline in revenues which in turn results in less game land acquisition and habitat development. This trend can also be reversed. If you have a friend who has given up hunting, encourage him to resume the sport. An invitation to hunt with you and your polished gun dog just might bring that individual back into our fold. Chances are good that your invitation will re-open a new dimension for him. While your friend has probably romanticized the sport, now he can once again become an active participant, thanks to you.

While we can all do something about bringing others back to our sport, it is crucial that we also help perpetuate it for the next generation. If the inclination is there, introduce your sons and daughters or other young people to the joy of civilized hunting. Teaching ethics, love of the land, respect for hard work, and the ability to clear one's mind of stress while in the field is a gift which will be cherished. Teaching young people right from wrong and showing them by good example has applications for sportsmanlike hunting as well as everything else in life.

In short, do something active. Don't be buffeted by the winds of public opinion. Show the public that hunters comprise class individuals who care far more than any other group for wildlife and nature. Do this anyway you can. Plant wildlife feed plots. Release birds into the wild. Train your dog to retrieve. Bring others into our sport. Work constructively with special interest and environmental groups so that we're allies instead of adversaries. Get politically active. Pride yourself in projecting a wholesome image through your good example. Join wildlife groups such as the Ruffed Grouse Society, Pheasants Forever, and Quail Unlimited, the addresses of which are found in *Appendix I*. Whatever it is you do, it will have an impact. Besides that, you'll still be hunting behind a finished dog and having all the pleasure and satisfaction that brings.

The retrieve is not an option--it is a requirement.

Photo 67 by: Dan Wizner.

Tittabawassee! We'll be back another day to enjoy great dog work, great company, and great sport!

Afterword

I hope you've enjoyed this book and found it both helpful and informative. The techniques presented here have been used many times with all sporting breeds during individual training sessions in which I specifically work with the hunter and dog together as well as during my training clinics and seminars. These methods are *tried and true* and will work for you also, provided you maintain confidence in both yourself and your dog. If you find you're not making adequate progress in a particular area, however, go back and re-read the applicable portions of this book. If that fails to shed new light on the problem, let me know your concern and I'll try to help. All dogs are individuals needing a custom approach to their training. Your dog is no exception.

By using the philosphy and practices advanced in this book, you've worked both hard and smart. You've accepted the proposition that there's no short cut for the equation:

patience + forethought + common sense + honest effort = a finished gun dog.

You've planned your work and you've worked your plan. Congratulations! You're to be commended. Your care, commitment, and dedication have paid off and you have a dog that will bring you much enjoyment and satisfaction. You have a dog that *does it all*!

Now put yourself back in the picture drawn in *Chapter 1*. Put yourself in your personal Tittabawassee Forest, wherever that may be. You'll have a good feeling about yourself, your dog, and your sport. You'll have it all!

Good luck to you in developing your own finished gun dog. The rewards you reap in personal satisfaction will be immense!

Appendix I

The following conservation organizations have done a great deal to support sound wildlife management practices which lead to improved upland game hunting. You can help continue their good work through your membership.

The Ruffed Grouse Society
451 McCormick Road
Coraopolis, Pennsylvania 15108
(412) 262-4044

Ruffed Grouse Society of Canada
RR #2
Glanworth, Ontario NOL 1LO
(519) 644-0855

Pheasants Forever, Inc.
P. O. Box 75473
St. Paul, Minnesota 55175
(612) 481-7142

Quail Unlimited, Inc.
P. O. Box 10041
Augusta, Georgia 30903
(803) 637-5731

Appendix II

The following organizations sanction field trials. You can write each one regarding rules and regulations.

The American Kennel Club Incorporated
51 Madison Avenue
New York, NY 10010

The Field Dog Stud Book
(American Field)
542 South Dearborn Street
Chicago, IL 60605

National Shoot to Retrieve
226 N. Mill Street
Plainfield, IN 46168

Other organizations also sponsor field trials. Consult a current issue of <u>American Field</u> for the name of a contact person. You can write or call The American Field Publishing Company (FDSB) at 312-663-9797 for a complimentary copy of <u>American Field</u>. The following are a few of the clubs which might be of interest to you:

Amateur Field Trial Clubs of America
American Bird Hunters Association
American Brittany Club
Continental Field Trial Club
English Setter Club of America
German Shorthaired Pointer Club
National Bird Hunters Association
National Field Trial Club
National Gordon Setter Association
National Red Setter Field Trial Club
Point and Retrieve Bird Hunters Club
United States Field Trial Club

Appendix III

We can all learn from others. The following magazines feature informative and entertaining articles on gun dogs, bird hunting, and related subjects. The first three noted here are available upon your joining the respective conservation organization. There is much that can be done by informed sportspeople who appreciate wildlife and hunting.

Pheasants Forever
The Journal of Upland Game Conservation
Pheasants Forever
P. O. Box 75473
St. Paul, MN 55175

Quail Unlimited Magazine
Quail Unlimited National Headquarters
P. O. Box 10041
Augusta, GA 30903

The Ruffed Grouse Society Magazine
RGS National Office
451 McCormick Road
Coraopolis, PA 15108

American Field
American Field Publishing Company
542 South Dearborn Street
Chicago, IL 60605

American Hunter
NRA Publications
470 Springpark Place, Ste. 1000
Herndon, VA 22070

Field & Stream
P. O. Box 52044
Boulder, CO 80321-2044

Fur-Fish-Game
2878 East Main Street
Columbus, OH 43209-9980

Gun Dog
P. O. Box 343
Mt. Morris, IL 61054-8088

Michigan Sportsman Magazine
Circulation & Fulfillment Center
P. O. Box 741
Marietta, GA 30061-9973

Michigan Out-of-Doors
Michigan United Conservation Clubs
P. O. Box 30235
Lansing, MI 48909

Outdoor Life
P. O. Box 51746
Boulder, CO 80321-1746

Sports Afield
P. O. Box 7164
Red Oak, IA 51541-2164

Wildfowl
P. O. Box 372
Mt. Morris, IL 61054-8087

Wing and Shot
P. O. Box 429
Mt. Morris, IL 61054-8085

Index

Aa

Airline crate 15
AKC..200
American Field 197
Attitude..52

Bb

Back casting..36
Backing 36, 103
Birds (used in training) 90
Bird release harness 69
Blinking...37
Bobwhite quail 223
Bolting...37
Brittany spaniel...21
Bumping...37

Cc

Cast..37
Checkcord 67
Chesapeake Bay retriever...................................23
Chukars..95, 226
Commands
    Bird..33, 79
    Come..................................28, 31, 78
    Dead...32, 98
    Fetch 32, 98, 100

Index

Give 33, 101
Heel 29, 32, 75
Hup 77
Kennel..15, 33
No 17, 32
Sit 29, 77
Whoa 29, 32, 77
Collar...65
Communicable disease..213
Continental breeds 23
Coturnix 92

Dd

Doves..227
Drainage 213

Ee

Electronic training collar 71
English setter...21, 204
Environment...210
Equipment...65

Ff

Faults:
   Bird-shyness...115
   Bolting 123
   Breaking point 147
   Bumping 124
   Catwalking..128
   Chasing birds 146
   Deed running...148
   Dropping on point..126
   Excitement over frequent finds 131
   False pointing...132
   Flagging 133

Gunshyness 112
Hardmouth.................................... 142
Low head and tail 126
Mousing.. 136
Nuisance barking........................... 149
Pointing dead 143
Refusal to retrieve 137
Running too wide 120
Soft points 144
Sulking.. 135
Trailing.. 118
FDSB... 196
Flagging.. 39
Forced Retrieving 39

Gg

German shorthaired pointer 21
Goal setting 55
Golden retriever 22
Gordon setter............................... 22
Griffon.. 23
Ground cable................................. 71
Grouse.. 220
Grouse dogs................................ 186
Gunfire.. 87
Gun-shyness 39

Hh

Hard mouth 40
Hip dysplasia 190
Honoring...................................... 39
Hungarian partridge..................... 226

Ii

Irish setter 22

Jj, Kk

Jargon 36

Ll

Labrador retriever 22
Land acquisition 232
Launch release trap 69, 70
Laverack, Edward 206
Lead 67
Llewellin, L. Purcell 206

Mm

Man shy 40
Marking 40

Nn, Oo, Pp

Parasites 213
Pelee Island, Ontario 224
Pheasants 94, 224
Pheasants Forever 235
Pigeons
    Training with 91, 191
Pointer 21
Pointing 83
Pointing dead 40
Pudelpointer 23

Qq

Quail.................................93, 215, 223
Quail Unlimited.............................235
Quarry...219
Quartering................................41, 81

Rr

Rabbits..231
Repetition.......................................28
Retrieving.......................................96
Ruffed Grouse Society.....................235

Ss

Self hunting....................................41
Shock collar...................................151
Shooting preserves..........................162
Shyness...158
Sight pointing.............................42, 81
Spiked force collar...........................69
Springer spaniel...............................23
Started dog....................................182
Style...42, 86
Style up..42
Sunlight/shade................................212

Tt, Uu

Tittabawassee Forest..................1, 2, 236
Train...74
Training table...................................72

Index

Vv

Vectors 213
Versatile breeds.........................23
Vizsla 23

Ww, Xx

Waterfowl................................228
Weather..................................177
Weimaraner 23
Whistle 67
Wild flush.................................43
Winding...................................126
Woodcock 222

Yy, Zz

Yard training.............................43

Order Form

Send check or money order to:

CJ Publications, 3260 Sheick Road, Monroe, MI 48161

Please send me _____ copies of *Gun Dog Training -- Do It Yourself and Do It Right!* ($18.95 each)

Your Name:_____

Company Name:_____

Address:_____

City:_____State:_____ Zip:_____

Sales Tax: Please add 4% for books shipped to <u>Michigan</u> addresses.

Shipping: $3.00 for the first book and $1.00 for each additional book

Amount enclosed:

$_____ ($18.95 each)

$_____ 4% sales tax for Michigan residents

$_____ shipping ($3.00 + $1.00 for additional)

$_____ total

Payment Method

Check or money order payable to: *CJ Publications*

_____Visa _____Mastercard

Account No._____Expiration Date_____

Name on Card_____

Signature_____